Designing and Implementing the Curriculum

Other Titles by Marie Menna Pagliaro

A Blueprint for Preparing Teachers: Producing the Best Educators for Our Children (2016)

Academic Success: Applying Learning Theory in the Classroom (2013)

Mastery Teaching Skills: A Resource for Implementing the Common Core State Standards (2012)

Research-Based Unit and Lesson Planning: Maximizing Student Achievement (2012)

Differentiating Instruction: Matching Strategies with Objectives (2011)

Educator or Bully: Managing the 21st Century Classroom (2011)

Exemplary Classroom Questioning: Practices to Promote Thinking and Learning (2011)

Designing and Implementing the Curriculum

A Compendium of Criteria for Best Teaching Practices

Marie Menna Pagliaro

ROWMAN & LITTLEFIELD
Lanham • Boulder • New York • London

Published by Rowman & Littlefield
A wholly owned subsidiary of The Rowman & Littlefield Publishing Group, Inc.
4501 Forbes Boulevard, Suite 200, Lanham, Maryland 20706
www.rowman.com

Unit A, Whitacre Mews, 26–34 Stannary Street, London SE11 4AB

British Library Cataloguing in Publication Information Available

Library of Congress Cataloging-in-Publication Data

ISBN 978-1-4758-3858-9 (cloth : alk. paper)
ISBN 978-1-4758-3859-6 (paperback : alk. paper)
ISBN 978-1-4758-3860-2 (electronic)

♾™ The paper used in this publication meets the minimum requirements of American National Standard for Information Sciences—Permanence of Paper for Printed Library Materials, ANSI/NISO Z39.48–1992.

Printed in the United States of America

Contents

Preface

It has often been said that knowledge is power. But knowledge is useless power unless it can be translated into performance. When teachers prepare for the profession, they take courses that give them a knowledge background. While that knowledge is useful, it reaches its full potential when it is not only implemented in the classroom *but also implemented well*. Even the best curriculum will be much less effective unless it is delivered with highly developed teaching skills.

Some argue that teachers and educators are synonymous. Others state that there is a difference. According to Sackstein (2016a), the *Webster* definition of teacher is one whose occupation is to instruct whereby an educator is "one skilled in teaching." But for Sackstein, this distinction is not enough. For her "a teacher . . . is someone who shows up for a teaching job every day. He or she knows the content and likely sees teaching like a job, whereas an educator is one of those people who goes farther than what is expected. It is the teacher who makes relationships with students more important than the content, but because of those relationships, the content comes alive." To an educator, teaching is not just a job but a calling.

Most people perceive teaching as easy (Labaree, 2008); but teaching is highly complex. Consider what Fryshman (2014) says about the complexity of preparing teachers, as opposed to preparing candidates for other professions:

> Preparing a teacher is in a certain sense far more challenging than preparing other professionals. For all its variations, the physician's focus on the human body is limited. So is the building studied by the architect and the court of law facing the lawyer. The classroom awaiting the teacher, on the other hand, is almost infinite in its variations. [There are] hundreds or so language groups . . .

vii

[there is] race, religion, sex, economic background, and age . . . variations in ability, in social problems—interest, physical and mental changes—the list is unending.

Every year our federal, state, and local governments spend billions of dollars on education, but this expenditure is wasted if effective teaching is not actually taking place at the grassroots level—in the classroom.

Over the past three decades, much research has been dedicated to determining what factors affect student achievement. One of the most significant studies conducted regarding what contributes most to student learning was led by William Sanders, a statistician at the University of Tennessee, and reported by Sanders and Rivers (1996).

Beginning in 1992, the state of Tennessee commissioned Dr. Sanders to analyze the teaching performance of its 30,000 teachers and the records of its six million students. In an interview conducted with Marks (2000), Dr. Sanders explained how he and his team examined class size; school location (rural, urban, suburban); ethnicity; students heterogeneously and homogeneously grouped; amount of expenditure per pupil; and percentage of students eligible for free lunch. Much to his surprise, he discovered that *teacher effectiveness* is 10–20 times as significant as any of these other effects. He was able to quantify just how much teachers matter and demonstrate that a "bad" teacher can deter the progress of a child for at least four years.

Wright, Horn, and Sanders (1997), in a subsequent study involving 60,000 students, came to the same conclusions. As a result, they recommended that the best way to improve education is to improve teacher effectiveness.

Sanders and his colleagues were not the only researchers to emphasize the importance of the teacher's performance on student achievement. Haycock (1998), working in Boston and Dallas, reported similar findings, with effective teachers having a profound influence.

The National Commission on Teaching and America's Future (1996) issued its influential report, which indicated that *what teachers know and can do is the most important influence on student learning.* Pipho (1998) concluded that the effectiveness of the individual classroom teacher was the single largest factor affecting student growth, with prior achievement, heterogeneity, and class size paling in comparison with actual teacher performance.

Nye, Konstantopoulos, and Hedges (2004) verified that what teachers do in the classroom has a direct effect on student achievement. Schneider (2015) reports research confirming that among in-school variables, it is the quality of the teacher that exerts the strongest influence on student success.

After studying in-service training and district innovations, Joyce and Showers (2002) determined that the key to the growth of students is the growth of teachers.

Despite increasing school safety, requiring uniforms, changing the curriculum, offering after-school programs, reducing class size, and increasing a lot more spending per pupil, Felch, Song, and Poindexter (2010) indicated that *the only progress that came in a chronically underperforming middle school was bringing in effective teachers.*

Hanushek (2011), in his own analysis, concluded that an effective teacher, which he defines as one in the top 15 percent for performance based on student achievement, can in one year take an average student from the 50th to the 58th percentile or above. The implication is that the same student with a teacher in the bottom 15 percent will end up below the 42nd percentile. And when assigned a teacher in the bottom 5 percent, a student in the middle of the distribution could fall to the bottom third by the end of the school year.

Hanushek's research also took into account student backgrounds and initial knowledge and applies to urban, suburban, and rural schools. He even goes on to calculate the economic impact of effective and ineffective teaching. Hanushek's study concluded that teachers in the top 15 percent (for performance based on student achievement) can add at least $20,000 of income *each year* throughout a student's life. In a class of 20 students, this teacher can add $400,000 *yearly* to the economy. On the other side of the coin, teachers in the lowest 15 percent can reduce this same amount *yearly* from the economy.

Economic and academic gains were not the only positive effects of excellent teaching. A study conducted with 2.5 million students over a 20-year period at Columbia and Harvard Universities demonstrated that effective teachers also had an effect on increasing college matriculation and reducing teenage pregnancies (Chetty, Friedman, & Rockoff, 2012).

If an effective teacher has the most significant influence on student learning, as well as on other positive influences, regardless of the background from which students come, then it is essential to understand what best teaching practices will have the most positive effect on students and how teachers can not only be constantly aware of these practices but also become proficient in improving them. This book is dedicated to identifying and developing the best teaching practices that will promote the success of all students.

Marie Menna Pagliaro

Introduction

Educational researcher Diane Ravitch (2003) provided evidence that peda-
gogical leaders have given credibility to dubious research findings *grounded
more in ideology than in data*. In addition, she stated that unlike those in
medicine who keep up with the latest medical research, educators do not
exhibit the need to know the latest educational research.

A significant problem in improving teacher quality is getting an effective way to have teaching research reach practitioners (Tucker, 2016). Even
when validated teaching practices that promote student learning are identified, few authorities require their evaluators to make accurate judgments that
these practices are actually being implemented. The work of evaluators is
reduced to assigning scores, which can be expressed as ratings, rankings, and
numbers. Teaching evaluation is flawed when the complexity of teaching is
transformed to judging behaviors that can be scored on a checklist, reducing
teaching to numbers, rankings, and ratings (Danielson, 2016).

Wiener (2016) emphasizes the importance of assuring that those who
evaluate teaching focus not on ratings but on how teachers can grow
professionally. Concurrent with the problems of getting research to teachers and proving meaningful evaluation is finding a way to give effective
feedback.

This book addresses the aforementioned issues. You will receive the most
current research regarding teaching practice, obtain feedback with respect to
your performance, and get information with respect to how you can improve.
You will acquire new teaching skills related to student achievement and
perfect those skills you already have. These goals will be achieved by using
the Best Practices Observation Instruments (BPOIs) along with explicit directions with respect to how to use these instruments effectively.

There are a myriad of instructional skills. Marzano (2003) synthesized them into three major categories verified by research—classroom curriculum design, instructional strategies, and classroom management.

These categories are covered in two books, which can be read in either order. This book, *Designing and Implementing the Curriculum*, focuses on best practices in developing the school curriculum. Foundational areas integral to curriculum development include understanding and applying learning theory, emphasizing assessment and evaluation of learning, and constructing optimal units and lessons.

This book's companion text, *Questioning, Instructional Strategies, and Classroom Management*, concentrates on best practices for developing classroom questioning (a skill involved in all instructions), using instructional strategies effectively, and becoming proficient at managing your classroom.

Since either book can be read first, the preface, introduction, and chapter 1 in both texts are the same. The preface delivers a framework for the book's importance. The first chapter provides the rationale for the BPOIs and an explanation regarding how to use these instruments to determine current practice in a relevant teaching area and then improve that practice.

It is likely that a vast majority of readers will already be practicing teachers. Therefore, instead of a detailed explanation of best practices skills, a brief review and update will precede the skills. This book would also be suitable for preservice teachers at the *end* of their programs, while student teaching, and as such, could also be valuable for undergraduates. Principals and assistant superintendents of instruction would find this text worthwhile in refreshing their own concepts of quality teaching and in helping their teachers deliver it.

To put the best practices skills criteria in context, these criteria will not appear as an isolated collection in themselves but *immediately* following each relevant review and update supporting the criteria.

Chapter 1

Becoming a Proficient Teacher

Learning even the most basic skills takes time, and developing teaching skills is a lifelong endeavor. A framework for acquiring teaching skills was offered by Joyce and Showers (1995, 2002). This framework includes theory exploration, demonstration, practice with accompanying feedback, and adaptation and generalization.

1. Theory exploration. As professionals, teachers must first understand the research that guides their practice. If you have completed a teacher-education program, you have already acquired this knowledge and will gain more when you complete this text. You can further explore research through additional readings and discussions with colleagues.
2. Demonstration. In this phase the skill to be improved or the new skill is modeled for the teacher. Examples of the skill in action may be conducted through written samples, a live demonstration by a peer or an outside expert, video recordings, or computer simulations. Teachers have often complained that in their teacher-education programs, professors never modeled or provided adequate examples of the practices that were promoted (Reiman & Thies-Sprinthall, 1998).
3. Practice with accompanying feedback. It has often been said that the three most important things in real estate are location, location, and location. It can also be said that the three most important activities in developing teaching skills are practice, practice, and practice.

The role of practicing cannot be overemphasized. Practice is required to develop any skill whether it is in the arts, sports, or teaching. You can do some of the practice on your own (unit planning, constructing teacher tests, rubric construction). But when your practice session involves interaction with students, it should be recorded through audio or video recording so that performance is documented.

Though you can practice and evaluate your own performance, *practice is more effective when it occurs with colleagues*. Teaching used to be a very lonely profession. When a teacher closed his/her door, s/he had to fend for him/herself with no input from colleagues, only an occasional observation and checklist evaluation from a supervisor or principal.

As soon as possible after the practice session, you should receive feedback regarding your performance from your colleagues. Immediate feedback allows you to become aware of parts of your performance that were successful and that needed adjustment. Receiving this feedback prevents poor performance from becoming routine.

When your performance is interactive in nature, microteaching, teaching a short lesson to a small group of your students, concentrating on only a few skills, usually not more than three, should be used. It is essential that the microteaching session be audio or video recorded.

Since a microteaching lesson is short and focuses on just a few skills, the teacher can specifically concentrate on developing just those particular skills and evaluating them readily. It is simple to count how many times they have appeared in the microteaching session so that subsequent microteaching sessions can document the increase of effective behaviors. Practice under microteaching conditions can then continue until the desired level of achievement has been realized.

4. Adaptation and generalization. There is no point in developing classroom skills if they are not actually implemented in the classroom. Once the skills have been practiced in a clinical setting with a small group of your peers or students, the skills can then be implemented with the whole class. Video or audiotaping interactive skills remains a critical necessity so that you can receive feedback for yourself and from your colleagues. In all cases, it is essential that you self-evaluate and self-reflect.

BEST PRACTICES OBSERVATION INSTRUMENTS

To address the issues of research-based practice, meaningful feedback, and evaluation for growth, you will be provided throughout this book with a collection of BPOIs. Each observation instrument (OI) cultivates a specific skill by offering a set of criteria for *developing* performance. The theory supporting each OI that follows was researched collaboratively by teachers, education professors, and teacher-education students. This theory is identified by the criteria (descriptors) listed in the OI for each best practices teaching skill.

The BPOIs coach and guide your performance and document your growth. Documentation is of particular consequence because it has been reported historically that there is a gap in perception between what teachers think they do in the classroom and what they actually do (Delpit, 1995; Good & Brophy, 1974; Hook & Rosenshine, 1979; Sadker & Sadker, 1994).

The BPOIs offered will empower you to take control over your own development immediately.

HOW TO USE BPOIs

BPOIs are easy to complete. After experience with the first instrument, teachers have often expressed how simple these instruments are to work with and how effective they actually are in improving professional practice.

To illustrate how to use the BPOIs in this compendium, consider table 1.1, Best Practices for Professional Development. The criteria in this OI, as well as those in all the instruments in this book, were developed by teachers,

Table 1.1. Best Practices for Professional Development (T)

Criteria (descriptors)	Performance indicators (examples)
The teacher identified reading for personal and professional broadening	identified *Classroom Instruction That Works* by Marzano, Pickering, and Pollock (2001)
read the materials and was able to describe what was learned	read text, learned that the nine major instructional strategies that affect student achievement are identifying similarities and differences; summarizing; reinforcing effort; homework and practice; using nonlinguistic representations, cooperative learning; setting objectives; generating and testing hypotheses; using questions, cues, and advance organizers
used the new learning acquired from the materials in the classroom	used similarities and differences when teaching verbs by comparing them with other verbs and contrasting them with other parts of speech
evaluated the effect of the new learning on instruction	evaluated students on a subsequent test on which they performed significantly better than they had before I made the comparisons/contrasts and just gave them definitions and examples
identified a relevant professional association (or associations)	identified the Association for Supervision and Curriculum Development (ASCD) identified the National Education Association (NEA)

(Continued)

Table 1.1. (Continued)

Criteria (descriptors)	Performance indicators (examples)
joined the professional association(s)	joined ASCD in June
participated in the association's activities and can describe what was learned	
transferred the new learning acquired from the professional association to the classroom and evaluated the effect of the new learning	
identified a mentor to assist in professional development	identified veteran master teacher Marian Floyd
identified others with whom to network	identified and contacted June Larson and Roy Pinzer from neighboring districts
identified ways to act as an agent to arrange for complementing my teaching	
collaborated with colleagues to obtain feedback for self-reflection	collaborated with fellow fourth-grade teachers Lisa, Tom, and Frank
used guided observation for self-reflection	used the Best Practices for Lesson Planning OI with my colleagues to evaluate my video recording
sought input from learners	sought input from class every Friday in both writing and in classroom discussion regarding how well the week went and what could be done to improve instruction on the part of both the students and myself
used a self-reflective journal	used a self-reflective journal to jot down what happened each day. Arranged with Marian Floyd to discuss my journal once a week
developed a portfolio for self-reflection	
As a result of the above,	
identified own professional development needs	
devised a plan to meet the needs	
If learning a particular skill/model was identified as a need for development,	
explained the theory supporting the skill/model	
If necessary,	
arranged to have the skill/model demonstrated by an expert or video simulation	

Criteria (descriptors)	Performance indicators (examples)
practiced the skill/model with feedback (under microteaching conditions where applicable) until a desired level of achievement was attained	
implemented that skill/model in the classroom	
evaluated the implementation of that skill/model in the classroom	
identified new areas for professional development	
discussed with colleagues if any changes (modifications, additions, deletions) were needed in the above criteria as a result of new research	

education professors, and education students after researching effective practices in professional development.

The OI is filled in partially to explain how to use the remaining OIs in this book. Before you continue reading, examine this sample carefully. Viewing it will provide you with a frame of reference and a context for the explanation that follows.

You will notice that the OI is divided into two columns—Criteria (Descriptors) and Performance Indicators (Examples)—and that some of the Performance Indicators are completed and others are blank. The column on the left lists specific research-based skills (criteria), best practices associated with that particular skill.

The set of criteria on the left are specific and observable. Specificity and observability give the instrument reliability (Wiggins, 2005).

The criteria describe mastery performance. When working with BPOIs, you should understand from the beginning that it is not expected, necessary, or in most cases possible that anyone can perform all the criteria all the time (Wiggins, 1998). However, since the criteria are determined because they positively correlate with student achievement, implementing most of the criteria will increase the chances for reaching all learners successfully.

You will also note that the criteria are not *necessarily* listed in order. For instance, you can join a professional organization before identifying reading for personal broadening. You can identify peers with whom to work before doing either of the above. In some BPOIs that follow in this book, the order will be important; in others, it will not.

The column on the right presents the Performance Indicators. The teacher (colleagues/evaluators) must put in writing in this column *exactly* how each criterion was actually demonstrated, providing clear, *detailed*, and appropriate examples. This process provides objective and more reliable performance data, making it easier for several observers (peers/colleagues) to agree that the performance has actually occurred. It is often also possible to provide more than one example of the same criterion. These examples should also be described.

Documentation of the examples is more focused and precise because the same verb and tense stated in the criterion are also used in the indicator. Verbs used in the Criteria (Descriptors) are expressed in the past tense describing what the teacher actually did, not what s/he plans to do.

For instance, the third criterion in the Best Practices for Professional Development OI is "Enlisted peers with whom to collaborate." Inappropriate ways to state the Performance Indicator would be stating what will be done in that category; putting a check, writing "Satisfied," "Completed," "Yes," or an equivalent term next to the corresponding criterion; numerically scoring the criterion; or offering an irrelevant example.

Appropriate ways of stating the Performance Indicator for the above would be writing the names of the persons who agreed to be collaborators next to the corresponding criterion such as, "Enlisted (same verb and tense as the one in criterion) Paul and Sally from my teaching team." Otherwise, the Performance Indicator for this criterion would remain blank.

Because the documentation is so specific, the BPOIs are more informative than the traditional OIs such as the commonly used checklist in which performance is identified in global terms and rated as an overall impression (excellent, good, fair, poor, achieved, not achieved, yes, no) or scored numerically with scale variations (1–4, 1–5, 1–7). In the case of analyzing teaching performance, this process offers little feedback regarding exactly what makes the rating of the performance excellent, fair, or poor, or what a score of 3 actually means. While receiving a reported rating (score) such as 3 for Average on any scale does give some feedback, this rating is useless in helping a teacher grow because it neither informs the teacher during the self-reflective process what "Average" performance actually is nor guides him/her how to improve in that category. In contrast, the BPOIs evaluate each criterion (descriptor) separately by identifying *specific* examples of each criterion in the corresponding box.

You have already observed that there are blank spaces under Performance Indicators in the Best Practices for Professional Development OI presented previously. Spaces that are not filled provide specific feedback identifying where performance could be improved. Table 1.2 shows how to complete the performance indicators.

The first session using these instruments provides baseline data regarding performance on that skill. From the baseline data, it can then be determined which additional criteria (descriptors) should be demonstrated or increased and which ineffective criteria demonstrated, if any are identified as such on an instrument, should be avoided in future performance. After obtaining the baseline data, the teacher can then practice, addressing only a few criteria at one time.

In their attempt to offer a teacher evaluation system that goes beyond using observation forms and changing them periodically, Danielson and McGreal (2000) have offered a blueprint with three essential attributes: the "what," the "how," and "trained evaluators."

The "what" includes clear criteria for exemplary practice based on current research; the "how" involves the ability of school districts to guarantee that teachers can demonstrate the criteria; and "trained evaluators" who can assure that regardless of who is conducting the evaluation, the judgment is consistent and, therefore, reliable.

The BPOIs fulfill all three criteria suggested by Danielson and McGreal (2000). These instruments express criteria for mastery performance (best practices) and help teachers demonstrate criteria by indicating which have and which have not been evidenced by identifying appropriate examples, thereby identifying areas needed for practice. The BPOIs provide a forum for "reliable evaluations" where the teacher him/herself must indicate *and peer evaluators must agree* which specific and accurate examples of criteria were implemented during actual performance.

Moreover, in the discussions of the examples among all participants, suggestions can be offered for *better* examples that could have been implemented. This interaction is professionalism at its best because it is highly effective in improving instruction and growth for all participants (Danielson, 2007). "Watching teachers in action, using systematic, validated observational approaches, allows trained observers to see very clearly what good teachers do to foster learning" (Pianta, 2007, p. 11). The BPOIs assist teachers and their colleague observers to ensure that agreed-upon researched criteria correlated with student achievement are understood and actually implemented in the classroom.

Using the BPOIs, you are now prepared to apply the framework for acquiring teaching skills (Joyce & Showers, 1995, 2002) introduced earlier in this chapter: theory exploration, demonstration, practice with feedback, and adaptation and generalization. You should understand why the criteria in the OI are essential (theory exploration).

Familiarity with the research and discussion with peers are crucial processes in assisting participants in both identifying and then internalizing the criteria. If there is a question about any criterion that is not clear, an example of the criterion should be provided (demonstration).

Practicing using the OI can then follow in a controlled environment. You may recall the old adage that practice makes perfect. Wolfe (2001a) reminded teachers that practice also makes permanent, so you want to ensure that you are practicing correctly.

As previously stated, microteaching can be conducted with a small group of your students. If you and your colleagues are satisfied with your performance, you can then implement the new skills with your entire class (adaptation and generalization).

Some BPOIs, such as one that may be developed for lesson planning, have criteria that can be demonstrated within a class period. Other OIs take a longer time to implement, such as the Best Practices for Professional Development instrument offered earlier and the implementation of the Best Practices for Unit Planning OI. OIs that take a longer time to implement are coded (T).

Above all, it must be clear that BPOIs are *dynamic*. These living documents are works in progress, guidelines whose criteria should be modified when new research develops. As more studies reveal different criteria for performance excellence and as new and validated strategies and criteria are proposed, collaborators should revise these BPOIs and/or develop new ones.

Also, it is essential to understand that a teacher can demonstrate all the criteria in the OIs and yet be ineffective. The reason is that teaching is more than the sum of its parts. There are always intangibles involved that can contribute to effective or ineffective performance.

BPOIs empower teachers to take control over their performance with constant reminders regarding mastery performance, what they actually performed, and what they could yet perform.

In conclusion, BPOIs

- expose teachers to best practices;
- offer a medium in which to internalize best practices;
- analyze present teaching performance;
- compare present performance to best practices by identifying skills yet to be implemented;
- serve as tools for acquiring new repertoires of strategies;

Table 1.2.   Completing Performance Indicators for Corresponding Best Practices Criteria

Correct completion	Incorrect completion
Use the same verb.	Use a different verb.
Use the same tense.	Write what will be done.
Provide a *specific, detailed* example.	Provide a general or vague example.
Provide a relevant example.	Provide an irrelevant example.
Provide any additional examples that may have been performed for the same criterion.	Use terms such as "Yes," "Completed," or "Satisfied."
	Place a check mark.
	Score numerically.

- foster communication and dialog among colleagues to continually identify excellent teaching criteria;
- provide a forum for discussing with colleagues more effective examples of criteria that could have been implemented;
- provide a structure for adjusting criteria and for creating new instruments when a new strategy and/or new research emerges; and
- evaluate the implementation of a strategy after practice.

Chapter 2

Learning Theory

A Foundation for Implementing All Curricula and Instructions

REVIEW AND UPDATE

The best way to develop your skills as an effective teacher is to concentrate on how students learn. To ensure that your instruction is as effective and efficient as possible, it is imperative that you are thoroughly familiar with the basic learning principles. These principles should be integrated into all aspects of your planning for instruction.

It is also most worthwhile to teach these learning principles to your students so that they will become more adept at processing new material and assuming responsibility for their own learning. Regular follow-through regarding student application of learning theory is important to constantly reinforce the way students are absorbing new material.

Traditional Learning Theory

Beginning mainly around the mid-1960s through the late 1980s, a large body of teacher effectiveness research was conducted. This research was predominantly in the soft science of psychology, sociology, and education. As a result, new learning theories emerged, and many older theories were reinforced. Some of these theories are presented for your review.

Motivation. Motivation is a psychological state that stimulates, directs, and sustains behavior. Motivation is the key to all learning. A motivated person learns better and faster and will overcome many obstacles to achieve a goal s/he is interested in and thinks worthy. The more a person desires to learn, the greater the probability that s/he will.

There are basically two types of motivation: intrinsic and extrinsic. Intrinsic motivation is the inner desire or natural tendency to do something. It is

11

performing an activity for the sake of the activity, especially when the activity is not required. Intrinsic motivation is self-sustaining (Deci & Ryan, 1985). Extrinsic motivation is that which comes from outside factors such as incentives (rewards) or punishments. The reward is not in performing the task itself but in the what's-in-it-for-me attitude. A task is performed because a reward will result for task completion or punishment for noncompletion.

Though many students come to school with the inner desire to learn (the ideal), the reality is that many others do not. It is then incumbent upon the teacher to create the motivation that supports learning by capturing and maintaining students' interest (Brophy, 1988). Interest can be aroused by introducing a little frustration (stress, tension), which throws students off-balance just enough to make them want to come back into a state of equilibrium.

The science of teaching tells the teacher that the right amount of frustration should be introduced. The art of teaching determines how much frustration is just right. Too little frustration leads to boredom; too much frustration turns students off.

Goal-directed activities. There is an overwhelming amount of research which shows that students who are aware of goals and objectives of instruction are highly likely to achieve them. When there is a purpose in learning something, especially when the goal is *personally* important to learners, they are likely to become ego-involved and thus succeed. Goals and objectives should be made clear to the students in every lesson.

Success. An old adage states, "Nothing succeeds like success." Learning tends to improve as an individual experiences success. Students should be provided successful opportunities, and the sooner the better. Make sure that the first activities you provide are those which will lead to success.

You can do this by introducing at the beginning of school some content with which the students are already familiar and new content in small segments after which the students experience satisfaction and gain the confidence to continue. You should be particularly sensitive to providing initial successful experiences for less able, emotionally challenged, and second language learners to give them encouragement.

Feedback. Feedback means knowledge of results. Students need to be constantly informed of their progress, especially knowing where their errors are. Quick knowledge of results allows students to correct errors before they become consistent (Elawar & Corno, 1985). You should note that students would rather know their answer was incorrect (receive negative feedback) than have no knowledge of results at all. Receiving no feedback is often perceived as receiving negative feedback.

Realistic and positive level of expectation. You should always treat students in a way that can assist them in reaching their potential. Of course, you must be realistic in what you expect the students to achieve and provide instructions supporting that expectation. Conveying the attitude, "You can do it," is likely to produce the possibility that the students will be able to "do it."

A student who expects to fail probably will; a student who expects to succeed probably will (Rosenthal & Jacobson, 1968). A positive expectation on your part applies not only to academic work but to behavior as well.

Active involvement. The more actively engaged the students are in the learning process, the better they will learn. Active learning is more efficient than passive learning and is more likely to promote long-term retention. The Chinese proverb (source unknown) states, "I hear I forget, I see I remember, I do I understand."

Use of senses. Concurrent with active involvement is the use of senses. The more senses employed in a learning activity, the better will be the learning.

Whenever possible, provide experiences that involve as many senses as possible. More senses will be involved if you provide direct experiences, rather than indirect experiences, with indirect experiences still better than vicarious experiences.

Example: Actually cutting a piece of glass tubing in a chemistry class (a direct experience) is more effective than watching the teacher cut the glass tubing (an indirect experience), which is more effective than being told or reading about how to cut the glass tubing (a vicarious experience).

Discovery learning. Students learn more efficiently when they are allowed to discover relationships for themselves (Bruner, 1966). Discovery helps to give meaning and deeper understanding to new learning. If students forget new information, they can reconstruct their experience they had in discovering the information to help recall it. Many teachers complain that discovery takes too much time. However, discovery learning is more efficient in that it leads to understanding (meaning) and, therefore, long-term retention.

Meaningful materials. Using materials related to the experiences of the learner is more successful in promoting learning (Gagne, 1977). Learning becomes more meaningful when it is made *personal.*

Readiness. Readiness means that students have the experiential background with which to connect the new learning. Readiness allows a student to build on knowledge they already have. A student who has never been to a zoo to see exotic animals will not connect to a story about these animals in the same way as a student who has had that experience. Teachers will often say that their students will be more motivated to read after a rich experience with that topic.

Students may not be developmentally ready for certain experiences. A student who cannot discriminate between C (an open symbol) and O (a closed one) is not ready to learn to read. This student will need more experiences discriminating different shapes and figures.

Sequence. Even if a student is ready for an experience, some topics must follow a sequence in order to be understood. A student who knows what a noun is has a better chance of learning what a pronoun is in a meaningful connected way. A student must know 2 before s/he can learn about 3. But *z* can be taught before *t*, and many other topics can be taught before others. You have to constantly ask yourself if the order of the learning makes a real difference.

Transfer. Learning has more meaning and is more efficient when it is *applied* to new situations and contexts (Salomon & Perkins, 1989). Learners must be able to recognize how new knowledge is applied or transferred to different settings.

Related topics from different subject areas should be connected with each other. For example, when studying the Korean War in social studies, novels from that time period should be read in English classes. Internet research studied in computer classes should be applied for the purpose of finding information in all classes. These connections give deeper meaning to the different subjects.

Part versus whole learning. In general it is better to learn a subject or activity as a whole first and then see how the parts fit into the whole rather than learn the parts separately before putting them together (Ausubel, 1963). For instance, it is more effective to read a chapter summary first before beginning the chapter. Then you can see how the different sections are related.

Part and whole are relative terms. What is the part in one situation can be the whole in another, depending on the developmental and cognitive level of the student. For a student who is first learning to read words, the word is the whole and the letters are the part. When reading a sentence, the sentence is the whole and the words are the part. The sentence is a part when reading a whole paragraph; the paragraph is a part when reading a whole chapter.

Early review. Most new learning is forgotten within the first 24 hours after the initial exposure. Therefore, in order to retain the new information, it should be reviewed (reinforced) once within the first day after the learning.

When students spend a short time reviewing new content within the first 24 hours after a class, they will learn the material better and remember it longer. Some ways early review can be employed in the classroom include summarizing the main points of the lesson at the end; assigning meaningful homework (not busy work) relevant to the lesson; applying the new content; and reviewing the main content of the previous lesson before introducing the next one. These reinforcing methods strengthen the retention of the learning.

Law of distributed practice. Short practice periods distributed over a long period of time are more learning efficient than one long practice session (Mumford, Costanza, Baughman, Threlfall, & Fleishman, 1994). Cramming for exams is a typical example of inefficient learning. Studying a subject a few minutes each day will yield better permanent results than cramming that subject the night before an exam. A student may do well on the exam but will not retain the information as s/he would through shorter review (practice) periods.

The same applies when learning a skill whether it is related to sports or to playing a musical instrument. Practicing a piece of music only 10 minutes a day every day for a week will lead to greater achievement than practicing an hour once just before the next lesson.

Choices. Learning improves when students are offered choices. These choices include not only how information will be processed but also how it will be evaluated.

Social interaction. Students tend to process information more efficiently when they are involved in peer interaction.

Recitation. Recitation means reading a certain amount of material and then saying what was read out loud without referring back to the text. Recitation has a greater effect on understanding and retention than rereading. Knowing in advance that you will have to recite after reading is more motivational because this knowledge makes you more inclined to concentrate on the reading. Reciting out loud gives you immediate feedback that helps you determine whether or not you have understood the material before continuing reading.

Interference. When two topics are similar, they should be studied separately with time in between to make the processing more effective. As an illustration, studying two foreign languages at the same time may cause confusion with vocabulary words and spelling in those languages.

Examples:

The word "cheese" is *fromage* in French and *formaggio* in Italian. Students often confuse the spelling of the first three letters, *fro* and *for*, and the fact that in French the word is spelled with one g and in Italian with two.

Since the letters *b* and *d* or *p* and *q* are similar in appearance, they can be confused by children first learning the alphabet and phonics. Teachers should, therefore, not teach these letters within close proximity but teach other letters in between.

Nature of original learning. The way new material is learned (encoded) is critical to how it is processed. When new material is "processed" in a confused or incorrect manner, the student does not have the option of pressing a delete button but must "unprocess" the material.

There are ways to assist students with learning the original material more effectively. These include:

Vividness. Learning is understood better and remembered longer if the original experience with the content is vivid. Vivid experiences gain attention

Table 2.1.   Using Contrast to Improve Memory

Present tense	Past tense
stop	sto*PP*ed

and have a greater impact on the learner. They include color, loudness, music, or physical activity to convey a message.

Contrast. The more strongly one part of a situation contrasts with another, the more likely a student is to remember it. Students understand and remember situations that are different, those that are exceptions, or stand out. To illustrate, the only word in the English language that ends in—sede is supersede. Knowing this makes it easier *not* to spell—cede words, such as accede or secede, with an -sede ending or supersede itself as supercede, which is commonly done.

When teaching the spelling rule that in forming the past tense in some verbs that end in a consonant, double the consonant and add *ed*, the students will remember the rule better if the letters involved in the change are enlarged and colored. See table 2.1.

Frequency. The more often students come in contact with the content, the better the chance they will learn it. Review (reinforcement) makes it possible for students to have more frequent contact with content; however, it is more effective if this review occurs in *different* ways.

Emotional environment. In order for students to be free to learn, they must feel emotionally safe (Covington & Omelich, 1987). Too much stress does not allow a student to focus on the learning but on distracting factors.

Varying activities. Learners have limited attention spans. Sedentary activities over too long a time period can make students restless and take their attention away from learning. Instruction should alternate sedentary with active physical learning.

Learning Implications of Brain Research

Beginning in the early 1990s, much has been learned about the brain. Brain research was made possible by advances in technology. Before this technology was developed, brains could be studied only through autopsies.

With the subsequent arrival of sophisticated scanning through positron emission tomography (PET) and magnetic resonance imaging (MRI), scientists were able to examine how living brains grow, change, learn, and remember. Brain research conducted by the hard sciences helped explain how traditional learning theory conducted by the soft sciences "worked."

The brain is a complex organ. To be a competent brain-informed teacher, you must familiarize yourself with the structure of the brain so that you can better understand the application of brain research. Once you are informed, you should teach your students how their brains work and what brain research has discovered so that the students will be able to apply this knowledge to their own learning.

Given space limitations, you should remember for the purposes of this section that the brain cells with which this chapter is concerned are called neurons. It is not so much how many neurons a person possesses but the number of dendrites (branches) the neuron contains. More dendrites on a neuron allow more connections between neurons. It is the connections that determine learning and enable us to perform higher-level thinking.

Neuroscientists have concluded that the only way we know that learning has taken place is through memory, and the only way we can get to memory is through attention. The brain is always paying attention to something. When teachers say that a student is not paying attention, what they really mean is that the student is paying attention to something but not to the lesson. Though students can process information peripherally without direct attention (Caine & Caine, 1994), this processing does not lead to higher levels of understanding.

The student's attention can be gained through the emotions, which are powerful attention-getters. Students can be reached emotionally by capitalizing on their interests and by making learning *personal* to them, their families, and their neighborhoods. It must be made clear to students what the content means to them personally and how it can be applied.

Emotions→→→Attention→→→Memory

Learning can also be made personal by using students' names during the lesson such as in math problems or in stories. Many teachers keep learning personal (and emotional) by displaying pictures of the students doing work or involved in special projects. Teachers who show their personal excitement for the lesson also have a better chance of getting their students personally excited.

Attention can be solicited by *priming* the brain. This means that students will note something if their attention is directed to it. Ensuring that all students know the objective of a lesson brings attention to the objective, giving the students an outstanding opportunity to learn the content.

Neuroscientists inform us that the brain is not designed to give continuous attention. Brain-savvy teachers who want to maintain students' attention keep involving them personally by making the learning more student-centered. These teachers offer choices in instruction and even in assessment and vary the activities by introducing something new (novel), whether it is new materials with which to work or a new methodology. Brain-informed teachers provide breaks at appropriate times for students to reflect upon and process new information.

In order to gain and maintain attention, the appropriate amount of stress must be provided. Too much stress (frustration, tension) and too little stress (boredom) both tend to shut down the brain. Think of stress as the tension on a violin or guitar string. When the string is loose, it has no tension. If in the no-tension state the string is bowed, plucked, or strummed, there is no sound and, therefore, no music. But if the string is tightened too much, there is too much tension on it, and the string will break.

It has been suggested that too much stress, whether it be at home, in the neighborhood, or in school, may be the single most impediment to attention and, therefore, to learning (Sylwester, 2000). High levels of stress produce chemical reactions in the brain that interfere with memory. Also, too much stress can lead to illness, which affects attendance and can lead to violent and aggressive behavior.

According to Sousa (2006), the appropriate amount of stress can be applied when teachers balance novelty (introducing something new) with rituals (routines). New activities offer challenge, and routines provide a comfort level that keeps students from experiencing too high a stress level.

Novelty can be introduced through enriched environments. Research reported by Diamond and Hopson (1998) has demonstrated that rats placed in rich environments, those with sensory stimulation such as bells, interactive toys, colorful materials, and ladders, developed larger, heavier brains with greater connections from one brain cell to another than rats placed in impoverished environments. Increased cell connections increase learning.

Moreover, Diamond (1997) reported that rats that simply watched the other rats interacting in the enriched environments, but who had no interaction themselves, showed no increase in cell connections. It is clear that learning is not a spectator sport. The rats had to be *active participants* to grow their brains.

Note that Diamond (1997) did not enrich environments of rats from normal environments and make those rats superintelligent. She enriched the environments of rats from impoverished environments and increased brain growth.

Jensen (1998) asserted that the hands are the most important "organ" of the brain, with the sense of touch creating important pathways to the brain. This is why interactive "hands-on" learning is highly effective.

Arts. The arts include music, the visual arts, and movement. Franklin (2005) described a heart and circulatory system lesson taught by an elementary school teacher who took students to the gym, gave them red and blue ribbons, and had the students form lines which moved in the same path that blood flowed through the body. Memory was strengthened because the students performed the activity physically.

In addition to offering a higher quality of life, the arts aid and support human development by fostering the growth of cognitive, emotional, and psychomotor pathways in the brain. In particular, the arts develop eight competencies identified by Eisner (1998) and reported by Sousa (2001).

These competencies are:

- the perception of relationships;
- an attention to nuance;
- the perspective that problems can have multiple solutions;
- the ability to shift goals in process;
- the permission to make decisions in the absence of a rule;
- the use of imagination as the source of content;
- the acceptance of operating within constraints; and
- the ability to see the world from an aesthetic perspective (pp. 217–18).

Another educational implication of brain research is the critical importance of understanding the difference between procedural and semantic knowledge. Procedural knowledge is "knowing how" to do something such as divide fractions or clean a carburetor—it is knowledge in action.

Procedural knowledge must be demonstrated. When faced with a fraction to divide, the students must divide correctly. "Students demonstrate procedural knowledge when they translate a passage into Spanish, correctly categorize a geometric shape, or craft a coherent paragraph" (Woolfolk, 2008, p. 242). Typing, making a bed, taking a shower, playing a musical instrument, and driving a car are also examples of procedural knowledge.

Rote rehearsal (practicing the same way over and over again) is appropriate for most types of procedural knowledge. Most of school learning, however, does not cover procedural knowledge but concerns semantic knowledge, which involves *meaning*.

Because procedural knowledge can be taught by rote, many non-brain-informed teachers make the consistent error of teaching semantic knowledge also by rote. A typical example of learning by rote is evidenced by completing a course and several weeks later remembering very little. Unfortunately, this is a very common experience. To encode and retrieve semantic knowledge, it should be learned through elaborative rehearsal.

In order to understand elaborative rehearsal, think of how you learned vocabulary. The purpose was to have you understand what the words mean (semantic knowledge). It is likely that you were provided with a list of vocabulary words and were required to look them up in the dictionary and write a sentence for each. Perhaps you had a test on this vocabulary shortly afterward. Subsequently, you probably forgot most of the meanings.

Wolfe (2001b) informed us that we are competing with a brain that was designed for survival, a brain that has kept us safe from predators. School-work, though important for cultural survival, is not important to the brain for physical protection.

LeDoux (1996) has demonstrated that with a brain that is programmed to forget what is not critical to survival—namely, the content we learn in school—we are at the mercy of our elaborations. Therefore, if we do not elab-orately rehearse, we will forget. Elaborative rehearsal makes learning mean-ingful, especially personally meaningful, by creating connections to what we already know and reinforcing the information *in several different ways*.

Example:

Give each student a different word; have the students look up the word in the dictionary; write a dictionary definition; write a definition that makes sense to the student (put it into his/her own words); create a visual (picture, diagram, chart) of what that word means to the student personally; put all of the above on a vocabulary poster; have each student present and discuss his/her poster in class; and hang all the students' posters around the room. It was demonstrated that using this method increased vocabulary retention 200%! (Wolfe, 2001b)

Methods *do* make a difference in learning.

Marzano (2003) described a current way of looking at memory. There is working memory and long-term (permanent) memory. Working memory contains the content you are *currently* thinking or reading about and/or are aware of. There must be sufficient space in working memory. When working memory becomes crowded, learning becomes more difficult, if not impos-sible. Since students can consider only a limited amount of information at one time, teachers should not overload the students' working memories. Teachers should try to judge the appropriate amount of content and pacing when pre-senting new information.

Long-term (permanent) memory is the huge warehouse where you keep the factual knowledge you have acquired: a caterpillar turns into a butterfly; George Washington was the first president of the United States; the hypot-enuse of a right triangle can be found by calculating the square root of the sum of the squares of its other two sides. You are not aware of this long-term information that remains dormant until called upon to enter working memory. Then this information enters your consciousness.

However, new content (from working memory) will not get into your per-manent memory unless you DO something with it—encode the information in different ways (elaborately rehearse). Research conducted at Vanderbilt

University and reported by Breaden (2008) has indicated that a 30 percent gain on a reasoning test was achieved by students who explained academic concepts either to their parents or guardians or who explained them out loud to themselves.

Other ways to provide connections (pathways) in the brain are through mnemonics, techniques to improve memory. One such technique is using an acronym, a word formed by the first letters of terms involved in a series. Common examples of acronyms are the names of the spaces on the G-clef, FACE (in succession), and the names of the Great Lakes (Huron, Ontario, Michigan, Erie, Superior), HOMES.

Besides acronyms, sentences can be used to help recall information. You are probably already familiar with the sentence or some variation of it used to remember the planets in order of distance from the sun, My very excellent mother just started unwrapping neat packages, correspondingly for Mercury, Venus, Earth, Mars, Jupiter, Saturn, Uranus, Neptune, and Pluto, and the sentence to recall the lines on the G-clef, "Every good boy deserves fudge (or fun)," for EGBDF.

Jingles, music, and rhymes can also be employed. Multiplication Rock was designed to help students remember single-digit multiplication. To remember the number of days in each month, you probably learned a variation of:

Thirty days has September,
April, June and November.
All the rest have 31 except February
Which alone has 28 and one day more
When leap year comes one year in four.

Any connection that can be made between new material and what students already know will increase understanding and, therefore, memory. As an illustration, in remembering how to spell "whippoorwill," it will help students to know that the word can be put together by combining three words with which they are already familiar—whip, poor, and will.

The types of associations commonly connected in order to distinguish between "principal" and "principle" and between "hear" and "here" are that the principal (a person) is your pal and that you hear with your ear. The difference between "desert" and "dessert" is remembered by associating the doubles in "dessert" with strawberry shortcake. Students who have difficulty remembering how to spell "separate" as seperate or separate should remember the correct spelling by knowing that there is "a rat" in sep*arate*.

Also, as mentioned previously, it is a good suggestion to teach students how they learn and how their brains work (Jensen, 2005). Thus, students can apply this knowledge in making learning more efficient.

What Is New in Learning Theory?

What is new in learning theory is what is old but with a new twist. The traditional theories presented in the beginning of this chapter, though over forty years old, have been validated by subsequent research (Marzano, 2003). What is new in these theories is some of the ways they are interpreted and applied. For instance, you already know that motivation is important for learning. Whereas in the past it was the teacher's role to motivate, now there is more emphasis on student self-motivation.

Marzano (2017) emphasizes creating students' self-motivation by giving them the opportunity to be connected to something greater than themselves and become more of what they believe the future might hold for them. In order to accomplish these goals, the teacher can engage students on several levels. First is gaining students' attention, then finding ways to energize them, next introducing intrigue, and, finally, inspiration. However, these goals are easier to accomplish when topics are studied in depth rather than breadth and when teachers are not pressured to "cover" numerous standards.

Dweck (2010) conducted research in which 400 New York City fifth graders were given a simple short test. Almost all did well. They were then divided into two groups. One group was praised for "being really smart"; the other was praised for "having worked really hard."

Subsequently, the students were requested to take another test with the choice of an easy one on which they were likely to do well or a more difficult one on which they were likely to make mistakes. Ninety percent of the students who were complimented for working hard selected the more difficult test, whereas a majority of the students who were complimented for being smart selected the easy test.

Dweck (2010) pointed out the difference between "fixed mind-sets" and "growth mind-sets." In the former, students either believed they are good at something or they were not. With this belief, mistakes underscored failure.

Students with "growth mind-sets" believed that some students are better or worse in some subjects but anyone can improve. Given this mind-set, students could accept failure better because it was considered part of learning (growth). Moreover, when students were taught about "growth mind-sets," motivation improved.

Covington (1992) discovered that students, especially those who operate on avoiding failure and competition, are highly motivated by being informed of their knowledge gain. This positive report on their progress, even if small, leads students to want to learn further.

It is also now recognized that one of the most potent student motivators is *choice* (Erwin, 2004). Teachers who place a high priority on allowing students to choose their methods of instruction and even assessments and communicate a trust in the students to make the best choices for themselves produce learners who become intrinsically motivated to succeed.

Csikszentmihalyi (1990) reported that when students are passionate about something, they will overcome obstacles to achieve. For a vast majority of students, there is at least one subject, topic, or activity that excites and, therefore, motivates them. Identifying this passion and capitalizing on it during learning will lead to a student's progress. For example, a teacher who knows his/her student loves baseball can use it to teach how to compute averages.

Long-term memory is best developed when the learning has *meaning* for the student. The brain is a meaning-maker and welcomes anything that helps it understand. Meaning is enhanced when content is organized, especially by using advance organizers, concept maps, graphic organizers and other visual tools (Ewy, 2003; Hyerle, 1996; Tate, 2003), and when fewer subjects are processed in depth, rather than in breadth. Gallagher (2010) reported that students scored higher on state exams when their teachers covered subjects in breadth; however, students who were taught in depth earned higher grades once in college.

Another effective way to increase learning is by using *narratives* instead of explanations. When appropriate content is related through drama or a story instead of just telling or reading, there is a significant increase in remembering the content over a longer period of time (Marzano, 2002; Nuthall, 1999). Telling about a battle through a play or a narrative is more effective than just telling about the battle or reading about it in prose form.

Moreover, Nuthall (1999) reported that students cannot learn content just once. They need *a minimum of four exposures* in order for the content to be assimilated for the long term. He found that these four exposures should be *different*, reviewed, and, therefore, reinforced in several diverse ways, with no more than two days occurring in between. The focus of these exposures should be on deepening understanding of the content.

Traditional learning theory informed us that feedback was important for learning. We now know that feedback and goal setting used together are powerful in improving student performance, even more powerful than either of them used separately. Also, the frequency of feedback obtained through assessments is positively related to student achievement (Marzano, 2007).

While it was considered that learning should be generally from whole to part, it is now evident that some students are field dependent and others are field independent. This means that the teacher has to present certain content in both ways.

We know that the use of mnemonics helps memory. However, mnemonics use realizes its full potential only after the students have a sound understanding of the content (Marzano, 2003).

Regarding the emotional environment of the classroom, it has been recently demonstrated that there are several characteristics that are conducive to promoting a positive classroom environment. These are having a caring attitude, setting high standards, and having all classroom members, including the teacher, show mutual respect for each other (Oakes & Lipton, 2003).

Weiss (2007) reported research indicating that carefully choreographed teacher gestures emulated by the students during relevant instruction seemed to increase memory of the content. He provides as one example the sweeping of the teacher's left hand on the left side of an equation and the sweeping of the teacher's right hand on the right side of the equation to show that the value on the left side of the equation should equal the value on the right. Having the students repeat this hand gesture helps them understand and apply the concept.

Keeping Up with Neuroscience

As you read through this section, think of it in the context of what information was presented earlier in this chapter. Recently, teacher-education programs have been criticized for not delivering up-to-date information on the science of learning. As a result, research conducted by cognitive scientists is not being implemented in classrooms (Felton, 2016).

In 2015, Deans of Education formed the group Deans for Impact (www .deansforimpact.org). They are committed to adopting and including in teacher-education programs the science of learning based on the work of Daniel Willingham and other cognitive psychologists. This group presented a document that is available on their website https://deansforimpact.org/wp-content/uploads/2016/12/The_Science_of_Learning.pdf.

There are five questions that the Deans for Impact has concentrated on. Each question has implications on what should be done in classrooms.

1. How do students understand new ideas?
2. How do students learn and retain new information?
3. How do students solve problems?
4. How does learning transfer to new situation in or outside of the classroom?
5. What motivates students to learn?

To answer these questions and be current in your practice, it is highly recommended that you visit the above website to download "The Science of Learning," a short document that presents the latest cognitive learning principles with their corresponding practical implications for implementing these principles in the classroom. When you go through the document, note what information and practices reinforce the content you have read earlier in this chapter.

You should also note that cognitive scientists have presented considerable evidence *contrary* to what you likely learned in your teacher-education program and what has been promoted in education methods textbooks. These contrary cognitive principles are:

- students do not have different learning styles;
- humans do not use only 10 percent of their brains;
- people are not preferentially "right-brained" or "left-brained";
- novices and experts cannot think in all the same way; and
- cognitive development does not progress via a fixed progression of age-related stages (Deans for Impact, 2015).

In his book, *Why Don't Students Like School*, Willingham (2009) offered principles of learning based on considerable research, not just one or two studies. Some of his principles are summarized by Young (2014).

Factual knowledge precedes skills and Background knowledge is important to how we learn well.

- Memory is the residue of thought. Students remember what they think about.
- Students understand new information in the context of what they already know.
- Proficiency requires practice.
- Cognition is fundamentally different early and late in training.
- Students are more alike than different in how they learn.
- Intelligence can be improved through sustained hard work.

Willingham (2005) provided a synopsis of his principles of learning regarding *modalities*:

Even though some memories are stored as visual and auditory representations, most memories are stored in terms of *meaning*.

Different visual, auditory, and meaning-based representations in our minds cannot serve as substitutes for one another.

Even though students probably differ in how good their visual and auditory memories are, in most situations, it makes little difference in the classroom.

Teachers should concentrate on the *content's* best modality, not the student's.

For Those Who Teach Middle and High School Students: The Brain and Teaching Adolescents

Armstrong (2016) has reported on research that neuroscientists have conducted on the adolescent brain that has implications for "brain-friendly" and "brain-hostile" practices in classrooms and schools. A more efficient brain formed by the process of dendrite trimming moves over the first 20 years from the back to the front of the brain. This means that the limbic system (emotional brain) matures several years before the prefrontal cortex (the rational brain).

Therefore, it is not until students reach the early twenties that the prefrontal cortex, which controls impulse inhibition and the ability to make good decisions such as planning, reflecting, and self-monitoring, is fully developed, leaving the brain areas that could control the feelings of the fully functioning emotional brain still underdeveloped.

Armstrong recommends that secondary schools should compensate for this phenomenon by stressing learning activities such as metacognition (thinking about how one is thinking), setting personal goals, working memory, planning, self-reflection on one's learning, and offering many opportunities to make responsible choices.

Though adolescents by age 15 or 16 are able to reason like adults, this reasoning can only be implemented when there is no emotional or peer influence. This is the reason that when under peer influence or an emotionally charged situation, students who are fully cognizant of correct driving practices will then go out and drive irresponsibly. And adolescents who can thoroughly explain the negatives of pot smoking will then turn around and smoke pot.

Secondary schools should offer real-life learning experiences (apprenticeships, service learning, internships) and peer-learning connections where teachers can help integrate students' impulsiveness with their reasoning abilities.

Middle school students, who are "in between," neither children nor more serious high school students, are more concerned about social status than academics, more suspicious of teachers and parents than in their earlier or later school years, and more self-conscious and emotionally sensitive than at other times in their development.

Armstrong (2017) recommends the following for middle schoolers:

Channel their energies through the creative arts (creative writing, sculpture, painting, choreographing a dance, drama, writing a song, etc.).

Teach through the imagination (imagining the scene in a novel, a battle in a war, the structure of an atom, the inside of a clarinet or an organ of the human body, etc.). These activities transform outward energies into kinetic mental images (sublimation).

Use humor and laughter *directly* connected to subject matter (humorous videos, cartoons, comics). Many of these can be found on YouTube. Assign the students the task of writing jokes, scenes, or funny stories relevant to the curriculum.

Table 2.2.   Best Practices for Implementing (Brain-Compatible) Learning Theory

Criteria (descriptors)	Performance indicators (examples)
The teacher provided all students with an emotionally safe learning environment	
ensured that students had mastered prior learning	
primed the brain by ensuring that all students were aware of goals and objectives	
motivated using the proper amount of stress by balancing novelty with routines	
conveyed a realistic and positive level of expectation that all students would succeed	
determined the interest/passion of each student and used this knowledge in instruction to enhance emotional connectedness	
employed a variety of hands-on vivid activities with multisensory stimulation (debates, role-playing, simulations, drama, challenging problem solving) and visuals (timelines, pictures, charts, advance organizers, diagrams, graphic organizers, semantic webs)	
employed discovery approaches to learning, when appropriate	
used materials connected to students' experiences	
ordered content in the necessary sequence (if sequence was an issue)	
provided opportunities for students to apply what they learned	
reviewed new material at least once within the first 24 hours of exposure	
provided short practice periods distributed over a long period of time	
introduced new topics that were similar with ample time in between	
exposed students to new content in four *different* ways	
offered students choices in learning activities	
offered students choices in methods of evaluation	
provided opportunities for learning through social (peer) interaction	
used mnemonics (acronyms, rhymes, rhythms, sentences, jingles, etc.), when applicable	
employed music and art to trigger pathways	
provided intermittent breaks in learning	
connected lesson content with other areas of the curriculum	
provided elaborative (not rote) rehearsal experiences to enhance meaning	

(Continued)

Table 2.2.   (Continued)

Criteria (descriptors)	Performance indicators (examples)

introduced patterns, when relevant
emphasized depth rather than breadth of learning
informed students periodically of their progress, particularly
  of their knowledge gain
used narratives to enhance content
communicated content by using that content's best modality
  (studying history as a historian, or science as a scientist)
encouraged practice for proficiency
evaluated whether students could state new information in
  their own words
evaluated whether learners could put new information in
  writing
determined if a student could *successfully* teach new content
  to another student
taught students principles of learning and how their brains
  work
checked periodically that students were implementing the
  learning principles
for those who teach adolescents, implemented several
  recommended brain-compatible procedures to deal
  productively with adolescents
advocated within the school district for positive changes
  in dealing with adolescents and the removal of negative
  activities based on the neuroscience of this group
discussed with colleagues if any changes (modifications,
  additions, deletions) were needed in the above criteria as a
  result of new research	

All adolescents need courses regarding how their brains work, how to use metacognition, and how to self-regulate their feelings when under pressure.

Research has also reported that the adolescent brain is more susceptible to stress because it is subject to the fluctuations of dopamine (connecting rewards and pleasures) and serotonin (connecting the brain to well-being and contentment). Implications for this situation include offering a curriculum that covers learning how to reduce stress, meditation, yoga, exercise breaks, and an extracurricular sports program that includes *all* students.

In view of the adolescent brain research, Armstrong (2016) offers suggestions that middle and high schools NOT do the following:

Teach mainly through lectures and textbooks. These methods do not engage the emotional brain and do not change the prefrontal areas of the brain critical to metacognition.

Post in public grades and test scores thus humiliating students in front of peers.

Lock students into a set college-bound academic program eliminating their ability to integrate the emotional system with the prefrontal cortex's ability to make decisions by removing their ability to pursue what interests them most.

Cutback physical education and recess in order to provide more time for academics which add to adolescents' pent up nervous systems.

The Best Practices for Implementing Learning Theory is presented in table 2.2. You should become thoroughly familiar with it. While it is not possible to implement all the criteria in every lesson, it is imperative that you refer to this OI regularly to ensure that when you and your colleagues are planning and implementing instruction, you make a concerted effort to use as many of the criteria as possible.

Chapter 3

Assessment and Evaluation of Learning

Section A: Assessment/Evaluation Background

REVIEW AND UPDATE

"Assessment" is a term that draws some negative connotations within educational circles. The reason is that there is often no distinction between assessments that occur daily and those associated with high-stakes testing, end-of-year testing, student placements, and teacher evaluation.

"Assessment" and "evaluation" are words frequently used interchangeably in the educational literature. For the purposes of this chapter review, assessment will refer to information regarding student performance *before and during* instruction. Evaluation will refer to information regarding student performance *after* instruction.

Assessment is the process of gathering information on student performance in order to make informed instructional decisions. The current trend is to determine first how you will assess what the students will learn before planning the actual instruction (Wilcox, 2006). Planning *high-level* assessments in advance will assure that you deliver instruction that will meet the assessments, thus giving you a mind-set to keep you focused on the key to successful instruction—student achievement.

Assessment information may be collected through a variety of formal and informal means (table 3.1). Formal assessments usually include the use of standardized tests, pretests, classroom tests, portfolios, and performance tasks, projects and presentations. Informal assessments include observing performance on homework and classroom assignments, student participation in classroom discussions, samples of student work, student feedback, student–student and student–teacher interaction, or performance on quizzes.

Information regarding students could be personal, behavioral, and cognitive. All this information must be collected to make an intelligent decision about instruction.

Table 3.1.   Formal and Informal Assessments

Formal	Informal
Standardized tests	Observation
Pretests	Interviews
Classroom tests	Quizzes
Portfolios	Homework
Performance tasks	Class assignments
Projects	Casual student comments
Student self-assessments	Samples of student work
Presentations	Class discussions
Interviews	Student self-assessment
Questionnaires	
Checklists	
Placement tests	

When examining table 3.1, you should observe that in several cases, formal and informal assessments are *not mutually exclusive* but can be used interchangeably.

Assessment is used to promote learning by providing teachers with constant feedback on the effectiveness of their instruction. Assessment serves as a rudder for instruction because if the instruction is not working, the teacher must adjust the instruction (change course) to ensure student achievement by doing something *different*.

Assessment is just as essential for students. It keeps them constantly aware of what they are supposed to achieve along with being aware of their progress toward that end. Assessment makes learning more efficient by concentrating their attention on what is important and encourages student self-monitoring and self-evaluation using clear and objective criteria. Assessment also promotes motivation by informing students of their achievement. Studies have shown that when assessment is a regular and frequent part of classroom procedures and the students are aware of their progress along the way, student achievement is higher (Bangert-Drowns, Kulik, & Kulik, 1991; Kika, McLaughlin, & Dixon, 1992; Stiggins, 2002, 2005).

There are three types of assessment: diagnostic, formative, and summative. Summative assessment is also referred to in the educational literature as evaluation.

Diagnostic Assessment

Diagnostic assessment is conducted *at* or *before* the beginning of instruction to determine what knowledge, skills, and experiences the students already have. The purpose of diagnostic assessment is to provide the teacher with input for initial planning.

This valuable planning information makes it possible for the teacher to know which students are ready for new learning and which students may need instruction before being exposed to new material.

Also, the teacher will be able to determine students' interests and which students may need instructional accommodations or need to work individually or in groups. Diagnostic assessment can be performed by observing and interviewing students, examining the results of standardized tests, checking anecdotal records, or by administering pretests or placement tests.

Textbox 3.1 lists general categories for observation (social/personal, academic, and behavior) followed by specific observable behaviors.

TEXTBOX 3.1. QUESTIONS FOR STUDENT OBSERVATION

SOCIAL/PERSONAL

How does the student get along with others?
What self-concept does the student demonstrate?
How do other students treat him/her?
What is the general appearance of the student?
How has the student shared knowledge/skills/materials with others?
What attitudes does the student convey?
How many other students selected him/her in a sociogram?

ACADEMIC

In what subject(s) is the student strong/weak?
Which subjects does the student seem to enjoy?
Where are there consistent errors?
What types of activities seem to engage the student?
What work habits does the student demonstrate?
What does the student do to demonstrate that s/he can self-assess?
What organizational skills does the student demonstrate?
What prerequisite skills necessary for present learning does the student
  demonstrate?

BEHAVIOR

How does the student demonstrate cooperative or uncooperative behavior?
Give an example of how the student follows (or does not follow) rules.
What acting out behaviors, if any, does the student demonstrate? What
  was happening in the classroom at the time?

Note that in all the questions in textbox 3.1, none can be answered just yes or no. Specific examples must be given to each question. What other questions would you add under each category?

Even the most experienced observers can sometimes miss noticing relevant behavior or can misinterpret behavior. Be sure that the behaviors you observe are consistent and that they occur under different learning conditions.

A way to determine student interests, as well as receive additional pertinent diagnostic information, is through a personal interview. The interview should be a pleasant, relaxed experience where the student feels comfortable, because students do not reveal their feelings in a tense environment.

Structured questions are helpful, but the teacher must be ready to explore further information (that can come from students) before continuing with the more formal format. For example, if a student says that s/he hates math, the teacher may want to probe him/her by asking, "What might make math more enjoyable?" even though that question had not been planned.

As you go through the following list of interview questions in textbox 3.2, reflect on which would be appropriate at various age levels and how the knowledge of each answer might influence instruction.

TEXTBOX 3.2.   QUESTIONS FOR STUDENT INTERVIEW

What are your favorite subjects?
What hobbies do you have?
Who are your best friends?
Which sports do you like?
What do you enjoy doing?
What do you not enjoy doing?
Which are your favorite TV programs?
What kind of music do you like?
From which activities do you best learn? (videos, lectures, projects, reading, learning activity centers, worksheets, manipulatives, other)
What do you do in your leisure time?
Do you like material presented in logical order or without structure?
Do you prefer to listen, read, watch a video, or work with your hands?
Do you like to be told a rule or generalization followed by examples, or discover the generalization after being given examples?
Do you prefer working alone, in small groups, or in large groups?
What is the name of the most recent book you read?
What is the name of the most recent magazine you read?
What questions would you like to ask me?

Now that you have read the list, what questions would you add?

You cannot assume that students will have answers to all questions. The areas in which they have no answers may provide you with teaching opportunities. For instance, you may want to provide hobby options as a choice of activities for a student who has no hobbies.

Though information about family is always helpful, probing too deeply in this area can be problematic unless a student voluntarily offers information. With increasing numbers of students coming from single parent and extended families, you cannot take for granted that students can answer traditional questions regarding mothers, fathers, or siblings.

Always remember that effective teachers are good listeners. Listening is critical not only while conducting interviews but also during *all* interactions with students. The old maxim states, "You learn more by listening than by talking."

Information gleaned from textbox 3.3 Student Diagnosis Form should help teachers perform an appropriate diagnostic assessment of students.

TEXTBOX 3.3.   STUDENT DIAGNOSIS FORM AS A GUIDE TO INSTRUCTIONAL PLANNING

Name _____ Age/Grade _____

Standardized test results:

Achievement

Diagnostic

Aptitude

I.Q.

Other

Classroom test results:

Relevant family information:

General health:

Information from:

Parent/guardian meeting(s)

Prior teachers

Learning preferences:

Exceptionalities noted (if any):

Relevant information from:

Observation

Interview

Samples of student work

General strengths:

Weaknesses in need of remediation:

General prescription for student:

Formative Assessment

Formative assessment is conducted *during* instruction and should be per-vasive throughout the class period. Formative assessment is a powerful instructional tool that determines the progress of students at all points during the instruction process. This process is educative with the main purpose to provide feedback, while the instructional program is still malleable by both teachers and students through continuous collection of information (assess-ment) regarding how they are meeting the goals and objectives of instruction so that adjustments can be made by both teachers and students to ensure success before it is too late. Stiggins (2017a, 2017b) has confirmed that there is compelling worldwide evidence that when assessment is used as both a teaching and learning tool, there is a profound positive effect on student achievement.

The purpose of formative assessment is not the comparison of students or the assignment of grades but to improve instruction on the part of both teachers and students, and students should be made aware of this distinction (Popham, 2008). Awareness of their performance makes students responsible for their learning by modifying their own learning tactics for the purpose of achieving an instructional goal. To reiterate, formative assessment is a pro-cess whose overriding purpose is generating evidence so that if necessary, teachers and students can adjust what they are doing to improve learning.

Sackstein (2016b) offers some suggestions for teachers to implement mean-ingful formative student self-assessment. She offers a list of questions and considerations that teachers can use to have students think about their learning.

- What do you think this assignment was about? Or, what was your under-standing of the assignment?
- What did you have to do?
- What steps did you take to complete the assignment?
- What kinds of challenges did you face? How did you overcome these challenges?
- What did you do well in this assignment? How do you know?
- Did you meet the success criteria? How do you know?

Wording for these questions will likely be adjusted for the age of the stu-dents you are working with.

The formative assessment process must be planned in advance, immediately after planning the objectives (chapter 4). The teacher must decide and communi-cate to the students what product or process (feedback to the teacher) will constitute evidence of student learning during instruction. Obviously, the product or process should match the objective. Would this feedback be a hand signal, quiz result, an exit ticket, eyes closed, completion of sentence stems, a written explanation of the content, and the like? For teachers who want to determine student engagement and achievement of objectives digitally (Plickers, pivotEd, Screencast-o-matic, Voxer, Kahoot), achievement of objectives can be gathered in real time.

Before a teacher can decide whether to make an instructional adjustment, s/he must first determine at what point in the subskill or building block knowledge acquisition toward achievement of a final instructional goal or objective this decision will be made. Before assessment feedback is received, the teacher must decide what will initiate an instructional adjustment. This decision is based on a predetermined minimum required level of both individual performance and class performance.

For example, a teacher may decide that each student should receive a minimum 80 percent achievement on a long-division quiz and that 90 percent of the class should receive this score. On the basis of these results, a teacher may include additional instruction or exclude planned subsequent instruction.

In gathering information for the adjustment, in addition to the feedback students give teachers along the way during instruction, the teacher may also use observations, classroom questions, discussions, performance on assignments, and student self-assessments (Popham, 2008, 2011). Once the teacher decides to adjust instruction, this adjustment can take the form of different input experiences, reinforcement experiences, student grouping, or any other adjustment method that makes sense.

Summative Assessment (Evaluation)

Summative assessment (evaluation) is conducted at the end of (after) instruction, whether that is a lesson, a unit, or a course to determine how well the students have achieved the goals and objectives. The teacher makes a final determination regarding what was learned by making a judgment on or assigning a value to student performance such as assigning a grade once the information has been gathered through assessments. Table 3.2 summarizes the different types of assessments.

For both teachers and students, it would obviously be better to know constantly how students are doing (formative assessment) so that by the time they get to be evaluated (summative assessment), they could improve their performance. Information for summative assessment may be obtained through classroom tests, portfolios, projects, performance tasks, and standardized tests.

To increase the opportunity for student success on summative assessments, teachers must ensure that before any unit of instruction (chapter 4) or lesson (chapter 5) begins, all goals and objectives are clear and communicated.

Table 3.2. Assessment

Diagnostic	Formative	Summative
Conducted at or before the beginning of instruction	Conducted during instruction	Conducted at the end of instruction (evaluation)
Provides input for initial planning	Provides continuous feedback so that instructional adjustments can be made by both teachers and students	Determines how well instructional goals and/or objectives have been met

Students should also be given the opportunity to preview and consider what the end products would look like and discuss together criteria for success.

A free assessment infographic that you and your colleagues can post in your offices or classrooms to assist in writing assessments is available at go.measuredprogress.org/what-makes-a-strong-assessment-item. The infographic describes seven key elements of strong assessment items. Table 3.2 summarizes the main characteristics of the different types of assessments.

While reviewing assessment/evaluation, it must be pointed out that the appropriate type of assessment must correspond with an instructional goal. If the goal is declarative knowledge—what students should know and understand (vocabulary acquisition or knowledge of cultural lifestyles)—then objective tests would be in order. If the goal is procedural knowledge—what the students can actually do as a result of knowledge (solve a problem or develop writing skills)—then a performance assessment would be appropriate.

Finally, if the goal is disposition development (interests, attitudes, and mind habits such as reflecting on experiences, knowing how to find additional information, coming up with original questions, or searching different viewpoints), then evidence such as student self-reflective journals, portfolios, or teacher observations would need to be collected over a period of time. It would make no sense to "measure" a student's persistence in pursuing work by a matching or multiple choice test question (Tomlinson & McTighe, 2006).

Section B: Assessing/Evaluating through Teacher-Constructed Tests, Rubrics, and Proficiency Scales

REVIEW AND UPDATE

Classroom Quizzes and Tests

As stated previously, tests are valuable in measuring declarative knowledge. Quizzes and tests differ in that quizzes are usually shorter in administration time and less comprehensive in content coverage. Quizzes occur daily, or after several days of instruction, and tests are usually given at the end of a unit. To ensure that your tests reflect best practices, it is important that you review the attributes of tests and create high-level tests that actually measure student achievement. You should also be aware that pre-prepared tests must also show evidence of careful construction.

Attributes of Tests

Validity. A test's validity is the extent to which the test measures what it says it is measuring. Does the test do the job it was intended to do? Does the test measure what students have been charged with learning?

Of particular concern to teachers should be content validity, also known as curricular validity. The content (curricular) validity is the degree to which the test questions represent an adequate sampling of what the objectives of the chapter, course, or instructional program were intended to cover. If the teacher spent more time on 3 out of 10 of the objectives, a comparable percentage of test questions (30%) should reflect those same objectives. Students often express frustration when a teacher tests them more on content that was not covered in class as opposed to content that was covered.

Reliability. The extent to which a test is consistent in measuring what it measures is its reliability. Is the test dependable, stable, and trustworthy? Does the test have scoring consistency from one measurement to the next? If the same test is given to the same student within a short time frame or to similar students, would the results be the same or very close?

To ensure reliability, a variety of measures should be collected on each student. These multiple measures would include not only tests that determine declarative knowledge but also a combination of performance tasks and products that measure procedural knowledge.

Types of Tests

Norm-referenced test. This is a test in which the student's score is compared to the average score (norm) achieved by a citywide, statewide, or nationwide sample of students. The norm is based on the actual performance of pupils of different grades or ages in a standardized group and provides a frame of reference for comparing students' scores with those of other students of the same grade or age.

Since the norm is a midpoint on a norm-referenced test, half the students in the sample group score above the midpoint (norm) and half the students score below. Though norm-referenced tests have some value for broad comparison purposes, they do not provide information about a specific student skill.

Criterion-referenced test. A test designed to provide information on the achievement of specific knowledge or skills set up in advance is a criterion-referenced test. This type of test usually covers small units of content.

Example:

Given a list of spelling words, the student will be able to spell correctly 8 out of 10 words.

Note that in this type of test, the skill is specific. The student must meet the criterion indicated (spell correctly 8 out of 10 words) rather than be compared with other students, and it is also possible for all students (or no students) to meet the criterion.

Constructing Classroom (Paper and Pencil) Tests

In this era of educational accountability, tests are being used for both assessment and evaluation. As soon as the teacher puts on his/her assessor's hat, s/he becomes a test preparer. And if the teacher is going to have to prepare tests, s/he should do the job properly and professionally.

Basically, there are two types of classroom tests: essay and objective.

Essay Tests

As with all types of test questions, essay questions have advantages and disadvantages. The advantages are that essay questions can test the types of objectives that call for the student to develop without suggestions or alternatives a response in his/her own words regarding higher-level abilities such as analyzing and solving problems, evaluating situations, or presenting evidence. Essay questions provide less opportunity for the student to guess the correct answer or take advantage of context cues and take less time to construct.

The disadvantages are that essay questions take a long time to score, have scoring that tends to be subjective and unreliable, and represent a relatively small sample of the student's achievement.

Suggestions for Writing Effective Essay Questions

1. Use the simplest wording to ensure maximum clarity.
2. Always word the questions to convey the exact task required.

Examine the following two essay questions to see if you can identify the difference between the tasks required.

A. Discuss the causes of the Civil War.
B. Explain how slavery was one cause that contributed to the Civil War.

The first question (A) does not specify the information sought. Besides using the word "Discuss," other nonspecifically framed questions begin with words such as "What do you know about . . .?" or "What do you think of . . .?"

The second question (B) is more structured and, therefore, more specific.

The student knows what to do (explain) to answer the question. Other specific questions begin with words such as "Compare," "Describe," "Summarize," or "Contrast."

3. Do not offer a choice of questions unless they are equal in instructional importance and difficulty.
4. Include just enough essay questions to provide ample time for the student to examine each question before answering, review each answer, and revise when necessary.

To improve objectivity in scoring essay questions:

1. Indicate for each question which factors will be considered in evaluating the answer. Scoring rubrics, detailed later in this chapter, will facilitate objectivity and reliability in evaluating essay questions.

Table 3.3.   Best Practices for Constructing Essay Questions

Criteria (descriptors)	Performance indicators (examples)
Framed questions clearly around a specific problem limited in scope	
Employed directions for responding by using terms such as "explain," "describe," "contrast," and "compare" instead of less structured terms such as "discuss" or "what is your opinion of"	
Communicated extent and depth of the response desired	
Corresponded to instructional objectives of the content covered	
Limited use to measuring instructional objectives not readily measured by objective-type questions	
Consisted of a larger number of short essays instead of one or two long essays	
Offered no choice of response	
Worded for simplicity and clarity	

2. Rate all the responses to the same question before rating the next.
3. Try to score all answers to a question without interruption.
4. Have the students identify themselves by Social Security numbers or by any other way to assure anonymity.

Table 3.3 summarizes the best practices criteria for constructing essay questions. When using the OIs that follow to evaluate different types of tests, begin by evaluating the tests you and/or others have already created for each type. These tests may have been constructed by colleagues or may have been obtained commercially. On the basis of the BPOI evaluated, make recommendations for improving the formerly constructed tests so that they will conform to the criteria (descriptors) for best practices. Be sure to first review How to Use BPOIs described in chapter 1.

Objective Tests

Objective tests offer the student the opportunity to give a brief answer in which s/he either selects or supplies the response. Advantages of objective tests are that they measure instructional objectives where writing skills *per se* are not important or measure instructional objectives best assessed by short answers. Distinct advantages are that objective tests are difficult to write well and take a long time to construct.

Objective tests include several categories: true-false (T-F), short answer (completion), matching, and multiple choice.

General Suggestions for Writing Objective Tests

To ensure that your questions are most effective:

1. avoid copying statements verbatim from references or texts;
2. if the answer to a question is dependent on an authority or knowledge of expert opinion, provide the name of the authority or expert;
3. construct questions using simple, direct language;

   Example:
   What is your reaction to the following T-F question?
   T F Nonorganic nutritious substances absorbed through ingestion are fundamental for the growth and maintenance of blood and bones.
   You probably reacted to the wordiness of the question.
   The question would be better worded in the following way:
   T F Minerals in our food help the growth of blood and bones.

4. avoid interdependence among items;

   Example:
   What would be the effect of having the next two questions appearing on the same test?
   A. What is the mean of the following set of scores? 85 87 93 98 68 75 82
   B. How many points from the mean would Patricia's score be?
   You undoubtedly realized that if the student makes a computational error in A, his/her answer to B would automatically be incorrect and s/he would be unfairly penalized.

5. construct "clueless" questions so that no one question provides a clue for another;

   Example:
   Examine the following two T-F questions:
   T F A histogram is a graphical representation of a frequency distribution.
   T F In graphing a histogram to represent a frequency distribution, cumulative relative frequencies may be used.
   An aware test-taker would recognize that the second question provided a clue to the first.

6. avoid patterning of answers. To make the test easier to score, some teachers may use a repeated pattern of responses such as DCBA in a multiple

choice question or TFFT in a T-F question. Frequently, the student can identify and even looks for the pattern. Did you ever do this?

Suggestions for Writing Specific Objective Tests

T-F Questions

T-F questions test factual information and do not test understanding or application. When developing T-F questions,

1. use a statement that is entirely true or entirely false;
2. phrase the question for clarity avoiding long-involved statements and qualifying clauses. When preparing a T-F question, if you write both a statement that is true and a corresponding statement that is false, you will have less of a chance of writing an ambiguous question;
3. avoid questions using the words "never," "no," "only," "always," "all," or their equivalents. A sophisticated reader will know that T-F questions containing these words are usually false. Avoid also using terms such as "may," "can," "sometimes," "usually," "generally," or their equivalents. A clever test-taker will know that statements using these words are usually true;
4. avoid using negative statements, especially the double negative. If a negative statement must be used, underline the negative term;
5. avoid using trick statements that have an insignificant error in the statement:

   The Battle of Hastings occurred in 1066 BC. The student may know the year but did not notice the BC.

6. keep the length of true and false statements the same. Because true statements contain more qualifiers and limitations, true statements tend to be longer; and
7. if you choose to use the modified T-F question, the kind that requires a student to change an answer if it is false to make it true, this question decreases even the chance of guessing and is more challenging. However, be sure to mark clearly through underlining, italics, or bold type the word or phrase that is to be changed.

   Example:
   T F The president of the Confederacy during the Civil War was *Abraham Lincoln*. In the above example, not only would the student have to know that Abraham Lincoln was not the president of the Confederacy but also that Jefferson Davis was.

Table 3.4. Best Practices for Constructing True-False Questions

Criteria (descriptors)	Performance indicators (examples)
Expressed statements clearly and briefly	
Wrote statements free from intricate language and qualifying clauses	
Focused core of question at beginning of sentence	
Worded statements as completely true or completely false	
Constructed to contain no trick items	
Worded statements in positive terms	
Wrote statements without the double negative	
Used statements that avoided clues such as generally, may, might, could, never, perhaps	
Constructed both true and false statements to be approximately the same length	
Highlighted part of statement, if student was asked to correct a false statement	

Table 3.4 presents the best practices criteria for constructing true-false questions.

Matching Questions

Matching questions are easy to score, need little reading time, and can cover a large number of questions in a short time. As in the case of T-F questions, matching questions are limited to factual information.

The matching question provides a list of premises (Column A) and responses (Column B) where the student fills in the response in the space in front of the premise.

Examine the following matching question:

In the space provided before each opera in Column A, write the numeral preceding the name of the corresponding composer listed in Column B.

Column A (premises) Column B (responses)

_____a. Carmen 1. Donizetti
_____b. La Traviata 2. Verdi
_____c. The Magic Flute 3. Mozart
_____d. The Flying Dutchman 4. Gounod
_____e. Lucia di Lammermoor 5. Giordano

6. Bizet
7. Wagner

Table 3.5.   Best Practices for Constructing Matching Questions

Criteria (descriptors)	Performance indicators (examples)
Constructed homogeneous premises and responses (all related to the same category)	
Introduced directions which expressed clearly the basis on which matching was to be made	
Presented premises and responses in relatively short language	
Arranged for clarity	
Used longer statements as premises, shorter statements as responses	
Wrote premises and responses that contained no extraneous clues	
Included at least two more responses than premises	
Indicated permission in the directions, if same response was allowed more than once	

Note that in the above question the following criteria were employed:

1. The premises and responses were short.
2. The premises and responses were arranged for maximum clarity and convenience for the student.
3. The basis upon which responses were to be matched to premises was clear. The wording could have been to write the number of the matching item in Column B to Column A, but the wording in the example question previously focused instead on writing the numeral preceding the name of the corresponding composer.
4. There was an unequal number of premises and responses, thus making it more difficult for students to guess the correct answer by process of elimination.
5. The premises and responses were homogeneous. All referred to operas and their composers with no out-of-context clues for correctly matching a response with a premise. If a contemporary composer of popular music such as Barry Manilow or Elton John or an artist such as Rembrandt were one of the responses, they could easily have been eliminated.

Best practices criteria for constructing matching questions are presented in table 3.5.

Short Answer (Completion) Questions

Short answer questions test specific facts. These questions may be framed as a question or as an incomplete statement.

Who was the president of the United States during the Korean War? _____
The president of the United States during the Korean War was _____.

To construct a professional short answer (completion) question:

1. make sure that there is only one line segment per single response;

    For example, when a student attempts to answer the following two questions:
    The gas we exhale is _____.
    The city in the United States with the largest population is _____.
    The fact that two spaces were provided is a clue that the answer in both cases above has two words.

2. compose a statement for which there is only one correct answer;

    What problems would students confront in the following two questions?
    The population of Florida is _____.
    Ernest Hemingway wrote _____.
    In both of the above questions, more than one answer can be correct. In the first question, a student can give a numeral; indicate that the population is growing older, wealthy, and increasing; or provide a myriad of different correct answers. In the second question, any novel or writings of Hemingway would be acceptable. It would be better to write, "Who wrote *A Farewell to Arms*?"
    How could you reword the first question (on Florida) so that there would be only one correct answer?

3. avoid questions with context clues;

    Example:
    An _____ is the part of speech that describes a noun. Using "An" instead of "A(n)" allows the student to guess that the response begins with a vowel or silent "h" if s/he was not sure. Of all the parts of speech, only three begin with a vowel: adjective, adverb, and interjection.

4. give the students a focus by placing the blank at the end of the sentence;

    The previous example could be improved to read, "The part of speech that describes a noun is a(n) _____. Using this phrasing, the student can begin to formulate an answer before reaching the space.

5. phrase questions for clarity;

    The _____ is computed by _____ the scores in a test and _____ by the number of scores. This question is chopped-up

Table 3.6.   Best Practices for Constructing Short Answer (Completion) Questions

Criteria (descriptors)	Performance indicators (examples)
Focused question at beginning	
Constructed all spaces of equal length	
Placed blank spaces at end	
Expressed statement clearly enough to produce only one correct answer	
Contained no grammatical clues	
If computational, indicated degree of precision expected	
Indicated units to be expressed	

and confusing. It would be better worded as, "How could the mean be computed from a set of scores?"

6. make all line segments of equal length with no more than two blank spaces. Look again at the prior example. The size of the line segments gives a clue regarding the size of the words to be inserted; and
7. in computational problems, state the units you want and the degree of precision.

If the length of a rectangle is 38 1/3 inches, and its width is 2 1/6 feet, its perimeter is _____ . The student should know if you want the answer in inches or feet and the degree of precision (nearest inch, nearest foot).

For the best practices criteria in constructing short answer questions, see table 3.6.

Multiple Choice Questions

Multiple choice questions are the most difficult to construct. However, these questions are also the most flexible of all the objective-type test questions because they can measure both factual and higher-level information.

A multiple choice question contains an item stem and a set of responses. The item stem can be expressed either as a direct question or an incomplete statement. The responses, usually four or five in number, contain one correct answer and the remaining choices as distracters.

The item stem should

1. state a problem or ask a question clearly and briefly including only essential information for solving the problem;

2. provide enough information to give the student a focus;

Example:
Carbon dioxide
A. is 20 percent of the air we breathe.
B. is heavier than air.
C. is present on the moon's atmosphere.
D. is available only as a gas.
This question can be improved by rephrasing it as follows:
Which of the following statements gives an accurate characteristic of carbon dioxide? It is

A. 20 percent of the air we breathe.
B. heavier than air.
C. present on the moon's atmosphere.
D. available only as a gas.

Note that in the second part of the example, phrasing the item stem as a question provides better clarity for the reader.

3. be phrased in such a way that the same words do not have to be repeated in the response. In the first of the two examples provided in #2 previously, "is" was repeated in each response. In the second example the word(s) "It is" were included in the item stem so that in the response, clumsy repetition was not necessary;
4. include enough information so that the question may be answered first without checking the responses;
5. be free, as in writing completion questions, of the grammatical clue "a" or "an" when using the item stem as an incomplete statement; and
6. avoid, as in writing T-F questions, an item stated in negative terms or underline the negative term.

The responses should

1. be such that knowledgeable people in the field would agree on the best answer;
2. be plausible enough so that a student cannot eliminate answers due to lack of knowledge;

Example:
The Italian who composed "The Masked Ball" was
A. Puccini.
B. Bellini.

C. Tchaikovsky.

D. Verdi.

In this question response C is not plausible because Tchaikovsky was not an Italian. Therefore, this response may be eliminated due to context, not knowledge.

3. be similar enough so that a student cannot eliminate answers due to lack of information. In general, the more the responses are similar, the more difficult the question. Contrast the following two sets of responses to the same question:

In what year did Columbus discover America?

A. 1100 A. 1412

B. 1492 B. 1442

C. 1630 C. 1468

D. 1776 D. 1492

E. 1812 E. 1498

You will note that in the first set, responses are so different that a student would have to know only that Columbus came to the New World around the 1400s.

In the second set, the student's knowledge of the year would have to be more precise.

4. have only one possible correct answer:

Hemingway achieved his greatest fame as a(an)

A. painter.

B. architect.

C. writer.

D. filmmaker.

E. novelist.

You should have been able to see that both C and E would be correct answers.

5. not include words or phrases used in the item stem. This use may provide a clue to a student who lacks the appropriate information. Note that in the following question, you will be able to select the correct answer even if you have no idea what the answer could be:

In the process of thermionic emission,

A. the positive plate attracts electrons.

B. a metal is magnetized.

C. kinetic energy is changed to potential energy.

D. electrons are emitted when a material is heated.

The fact that "emission" was used in the item stem and "emitted" was used as one of the item responses made it easy to select D as the correct answer.

6. provide an appropriate number of choices for the grade level (in general, two to three choices for second graders, three to four choices for third and fourth graders, and four or more for older students);

7. avoid overlapping;

Example:

How many U.S. presidents were lawyers?

A. Fewer than 5

B. Fewer than 8

C. More than 8

D. More than 10

More than one response would be correct.

8. avoid "none of these" as an alternative unless the response can be expressed in exact terms;

Barbara has 10 nickels, 3 quarters, 5 dimes, and 8 pennies. How much money does she have?

A. $1.53

B. $1.62

C. $1.87

D. None of these

Also, if a student knows that only one of the answers is correct in any question, s/he could eliminate "none of these" as a response.

9. avoid "all of the above." The student can eliminate "all of the above" by knowing that only one of the other answers was incorrect.

To format clear and consistent multiple choice questions:

1. use small or capital letters instead of numerals for responses. Since the questions themselves are generally listed as numerals, employing letters as responses is less confusing;

2. place the letters corresponding to the responses directly beneath the beginning of the item stem;

3. if the item stem is a direct question, capitalize the first word of each response. If the item stem is an incomplete sentence, do not capitalize the first word of each response, and place a period at the end of each response;
4. if the responses are numerals,

    A. arrange the responses from smallest to largest;
    B. when working with decimals, place decimal points one underneath the other and use the same number of decimal places; and
    C. when using dollar signs, place the dollars signs one underneath the other.

5. use a random process for locating responses.

See table 3.7 for best practices criteria in constructing multiple choice questions.

Students are currently being assisted in becoming lifelong learners who assume more responsibility for their own learning. As part of the assessment/evaluation process, students should participate in constructing tests.

Table 3.7.   Best Practices for Constructing Multiple Choice Questions

Criteria (descriptors)	Performance indicators (examples)
Item stems	
Framed as a question or incomplete statement	
Expressed with only one central problem	
Expressed clearly	
Contained no extraneous clues	
Contained no negative statements or highlighted negative statements	
Expressed so that no words in the premise were repeated in the response	
Offered only one correct response	
Provided enough information so that students could formulate an answer before examining choices	
Responses	
Offered mutually exclusive choices	
Offered all plausible and attractive choices	
Written grammatically consistently with item stem	
Expressed with parallel construction	
Arranged in logical order, when appropriate	
Located at the ends of questions or incomplete statements	
Employed "none of these" only when the answer could be expressed in exact terms	
Excluded "all of the above" as a choice	
Tested items so that experts in the field could agree on the correct answer	

Think of what it takes to develop a test. First the material must be mastered in depth. Then the content must be manipulated in different ways to construct test questions. Students can develop questions as a culminating activity, administer the test to other students, and check each other's work. The situation can also be *reversed* so that students can also be provided with answers to tests and then design questions that will elicit those answers.

Test construction is an excellent way for students to review a chapter or a unit. You can teach them, depending on their age and grade level, what you reviewed in this chapter about designing tests. You can also have students analyze test questions to see how they meet the criteria described in this chapter. If you model professional test construction, your students will have a better opportunity to design professional test questions themselves.

Performance Tasks and Products

Performance tasks and products provide alternative assessment techniques, often referred to in the educational literature as performance assessment or authentic assessment. As opposed to completing tests, students must show that they can *do* something as a result of knowledge gained when they are involved in authentic assessments.

In performance assessment students must *generate* rather than select a response. "Products guide students in moving from consumers *of* knowledge to producers *with* knowledge" (Tomlinson & Eidson, 2003, p. 11, italics in the original).

Students are actually performing a designated activity to demonstrate competence (Mitchell, 1992). These performance projects provide high-level challenges representing problems that must be faced in the "real world" (authentic) outside of school and make school more relevant by engaging students in meaningful applications. The level of complexity of the task depends on the student's stage of development.

Meyer (1992) pointed out that the terms, "performance tasks" and "authentic tasks," are often used interchangeably. Though both require that students come up with their own responses and apply knowledge, performance tasks tend to be more contrived. For a task or product to be authentic, all the following attributes must be present:

1. The student must perform the subject as opposed to just talking or reporting about it.
2. The task or product must be one representing a real-life situation, whether it is solving a problem confronted in personal life, as a citizen, or in the work environment.
3. The student must apply knowledge and skills by solving a previously unsolved problem.

Table 3.8. Examples of Tasks and Products

Task	Product
Analyzing a budget using specific criteria	Creating an original budget using the same criteria
Comparing and contrasting two battles in a war	Designing a strategy to make the losing battle the winning one

4. The student must integrate a repertoire of knowledge and skills in the application.
5. Guidelines, standards, resources, and adequate feedback must be provided so that the student may self-adjust.
6. The task should be about something important.
7. The task must be challenging for the present level of student performance.

Though tasks and products are used synonymously, there are subtle differences between the two with the product being more advanced. See table 3.8.

Tasks and products are not the same as instructional activities. An instructional activity is designed to *learn* one or more objectives. Tasks and products are designed to *assess* the extent and level to which the objectives (achievement targets) have been mastered. Threading a sewing machine is an activity, which teaches a student how to thread; redesigning the machine to make the threading more efficient is a task; building the redesigned machine and then organizing a marketing strategy to promote it would be a product.

For a task or product to be valid, it must be one that demonstrates achievement of the goals of instruction. There are many tasks that may meet the criterion of authenticity, but if they do not assess how the students have met the objectives of a chapter or unit, the tasks do not meet the criterion of validity.

Student Portfolios

A student portfolio is a collection over time of student work that documents progress. A portfolio is not just any collection of work placed into a folder. In order to have maximum worth as an assessment tool, the purpose of the portfolio must be perfectly clear to both teacher and student. The purpose determines what is to be collected, which criteria will be used to review the collection, and how the portfolio will be scored.

Teacher and student are active in the process of portfolio evaluation in which they decide together what work may be used, removed, or added as the process of portfolio development continues so that it may produce valid, reliable evidence of achievement.

Danielson and Abrutyn (1997) suggested that students spend time sharing portfolios.

The portfolio may serve as a

- capstone project, the crowning achievement produced by a student;
- display or showcase project used for a professional to make a judgment, such as a collection of the best art projects for submission to an art school for program admission;
- sample of the student's best work;
- sample of student growth; and
- sample of the student's ability to self-assess and improve performance.

Constructing Rubrics for Performance Tasks, Products, and Portfolios

Performance tasks, products, and portfolios achieve full potential when they are accompanied by scoring rubrics. A scoring rubric is a set of criteria for judging performance. In a scoring rubric, the criteria (descriptors) are arranged in a hierarchy that ranges from the poorest to the best performance. Scoring rubrics allow teachers and students to judge or rate student performance objectively. If scoring rubrics are constructed well, they also have the critical function of allowing students to self-assess their work and, as a result, self-adjust and improve.

Teachers and students sometimes get so involved with the assessment component in a rubric that they forget that the rubric is an important *teaching tool*. It offers criteria that allow students to move to higher levels of achievement.

Scoring rubrics contain "an identified behavior within an assessment task; quality or performance standard; description of the desired standard; and a scale to be used in rating student performance" (Taggert, Phifer, Nixon, & Wood, 1998, pp. 58–59). Before a scoring rubric can be constructed, the person who prepares it must determine what constitutes quality performance in a representative work.

Wiggins and McTighe (1998, 2005), two leaders in the field of assessment, suggested that samples of students' and professionals' work should be analyzed first to determine what range of excellence they demonstrate. It is essential that rubrics be constructed on the basis of the absolute best possible performance, because if they are constructed the way students are currently performing, the students will remain at that performance level.

Once the best performance is determined, then minimal performance should be identified. After both the poorest and best performances are described, intermediate levels between the two are determined, and a scoring rubric can then be presented quantitatively as a scale. The scale can range from 1 to 4 or 1 to 10, with the most common scoring rubric presenting a scale from 1 to 6, with 1 as the lowest level of performance and 6 the highest.

Scoring rubrics may also be expressed qualitatively as poor through outstanding, novice through professional, emergent through fluent, or any other equivalent system depending on the type of performance being assessed. It is recommended that the number of categories in the quantitative or qualitative scale be *even* because judgment tends toward the center. If a scale of 1–5 is used, many evaluators, even with specific criteria, will tend to select the midpoint, 3.

To illustrate, examine textbox 3.4, Map Legend for Scoring Rubrics.

Decide whether in textbox 3.4, which offers an odd number of levels, the tendency might lead to selecting Level 2 (Complex) because it is in the middle (between 1 and 3).

Corresponding to each point or level on a scale is a set of performance descriptors that indicates clearly what criteria must be demonstrated to qualify for that score. Criteria should always be described in *positive* terms, what the performance was, instead of what the performance was not. It would be a better-stated descriptor as, "made basic computational errors," as opposed to, "did not have the ability to compute basic problems."

The criteria should not be evaluative (fair, good, excellent) and should discriminate sufficiently from each other so that each level of achievement can be distinguished with no overlapping. Clear, discriminating criteria give validity to a rubric. You have already read in chapter 1 that specificity and observability give reliability to a rubric.

As mentioned previously, using a well-prepared scoring rubric to grade essay questions would give the scoring validity and higher reliability (Wiggins, 2005).

Wiggins and McTighe (2005) asserted that the rubric should be written *before* deciding what task or product to assign. The criteria identified in the rubric would be able to guide the selection of the task that would best provide

---

**TEXTBOX 3.4.   MAP LEGEND FOR
SCORING RUBRICS**

Level 3 (Higher Order): creates an original legend to communicate spatial arrangements and directions
Level 2 (Complex): interprets map subtleties that go beyond just reading the legend
Level 1 (Basic): states literal meanings of legend items (Adapted from Lazear [1998, p. 56])

Table 3.9.   Best Practices for Constructing Scoring Rubrics

Criteria (descriptors)	Performance indicators (examples)
Analyzed a wide range of work samples before determining criteria for assessing the task	
Described the performance extremes before determining criteria	
Expressed performance criteria in clear, descriptive language free of evaluative terms	
Differentiated clearly among performance levels so that students can self-assess and self-correct	
Stated criteria in positive terms at all levels	
Presented an *even* number of quantitative or qualitative levels	
Designed criteria with student input, when appropriate	
Presented rubric and discussed criteria with students *before* they began to work on task or product	

the opportunity for meeting the criteria. See table 3.9 for the best practices criteria for constructing scoring rubrics.

Many educators believe that when the students are developmentally ready, they should *participate in creating* the rubric so that the criteria can be internalized. Regardless of whether or not students participate in rubric construction, it is essential that they are presented with the rubric *before* they begin working on a task, product, or portfolio and that they are clear regarding the meaning of each criterion.

Proficiency Scales

Marzano (2017) notes that while rubrics are valuable, they are limited to providing *specific* information on assessing student knowledge of or performance on one task. He recommends that educators shift from an assessment perspective to one of measurement. To focus on measurement, Marzano promotes the use of proficiency scales, which are more general than rubrics and describe the progression of knowledge or skill to be achieved, thus providing students with explicit feedback.

Using a scale, the student knows where s/he is along the scale and what must be achieved to progress to the next level. As students observe their progress on the scale, they become more motivated because they see their knowledge gain (chapter 2). Explicit knowledge from a proficiency scale as to what knowledge they have or have not attained is more valuable to students than receiving grades and/or a series of independent assessments. For this reason, it has been suggested that proficiency scales can be used as report cards.

Marzano believes that teachers or districts should unpack standards and decide on a small set of topics for each content area and grade level. Then it would best be on a *district level* that proficiency scales reflecting this content be created. Along with the content on the scale level, an assessment should be constructed that corresponds with that level of content complexity.

To assist teachers and district in facilitating the process of creating proficiency scales, Dr. Marzano has offered a valuable Proficiency Scale Bank at http://www.marzanoresearch.com. Click on Free Resources and then on Proficiency Scale Bank. Type in the particular standard in which you are interested, and you should receive a proficiency scale for that standard. You will note that scales range from 0.0 to 4.0 separated by 0.5 intervals. These half-point scores indicate partial success on the way to higher levels.

Figure 3.1 is a sample proficiency scale. For your convenience, an additional column has been added to explain the different content/skill score levels.

	The student will be able to	*Explanation of 4.0, 3.0, and 2.0 scores*
4.0	compare the angle sums of triangles to the sums of other polygons	apply knowledge and demonstrate in-depth content/skill exceeding what was taught
3.5	In addition to score 3.0 performance, the student has partial success at score 4.0 content	
3.0	explain the relationships among the angles of triangles, including the sum of interior angles and angle to angle similarity	perform the task with no major errors or omissions
2.5	The student has no major errors or omissions regarding score 2.0 content and partial success at score 3.0 content	
2.0	state that the measures of the interior angles of a triangle add up to 180 degrees; explain conditions for corresponding angles of two triangles to be congruent and similar; demonstrate interior and exterior angles; define angle sum, corresponding angles, congruence, and similarity; distinguish between regular and irregular polygons; define a polygon; and give examples and nonexamples of polygons	recognize or recall foundational (prerequisite) content/skills without major errors while still exhibiting major errors or omissions regarding the more complex ideas and processes
1.5	The student has partial success at score 2.0 content but major errors/omissions regarding 3.0 content	
1.0	With assistance, the student has partial success at score 2.0 content and score 3.0 content	
0.5	With assistance, the student has partial success at score 2.0 content but not score 3.0 content	
0.0	Even with assistance, the student has no success	

Figure 3.1.   Polygon angle sums

Table 3.10.   Best Practices for Creating a Proficiency Scale

Criteria (descriptors)	Performance indicators (examples)
Identified the standard to be addressed	
Unpacked the standard (what students should know and be able to do)	
Selected the most important (essential) content/skills	
Collaborated with colleagues on a district level to create a proficiency scale to communicate acquisition of the most important content/skills for that standard or used a proficiency scale prepared by the district	
Constructed a scale from 0.0 to 4.0 separated by 0.5 intervals	
Identified the lowest content/skill acquisition level at score 2.0	
Identified the next higher content/skill acquisition level at score 3.0	
Identified the highest content/skill acquisition level at score 4.0	
Designed an assessment for levels 2.0, 3.0, and 4.0	
Distributed the proficiency scale to students	
Asked students to rewrite in their own words the content/skill targets in levels 2.0, 3.0, and 4.0	
Asked students to design their own assessments for target levels 2.0, 3.0, and 4.0	
Communicated to the students in levels 0.0 through 1.5 and in levels 2.5 and 3.5 their progress on the way to achieving levels 2.0, 3.0, and 4.0	

Marzano (2017) also recommends that teachers post relevant proficiency scales at the beginning of a unit and discuss how the unit goals coordinate with the tasks described on the scale. To internalize the scale, students should be encouraged to rewrite in their own words the learning descriptions for levels 2.0, 3.0, and 4.0 and explain these levels. Then students should construct their own assessments for each level.

Before beginning a lesson, teachers can show how the lesson is designed to achieve one or more related tasks on a proficiency scale.

The BPOI for creating proficiency scales is presented in table 3.10.

Chapter 4

Proficient Unit Planning

REVIEW AND UPDATE

Madeline Hunter, who contributed so much to applying research to lesson planning, later reflected that if she had to do it over again, she would have concentrated on unit planning rather than on lesson planning. She is quoted as saying that she saw lessons as fluctuating too much each day, with units giving an important overall guide and focus to instruction (Marzano, 2002). This chapter reviews unit planning first because it provides a context and framework from which to plan individual lessons (chapter 5).

When planning units, it is important to distinguish the difference between curriculum and instruction. There are several different ways to define "curriculum," but for the purposes of this review, curriculum is concerned with *what* specifically will be taught within a subject or content area. Instruction focuses on *how* that content is taught or what methods (input) will be used to best convey the content. Both curriculum and instruction decisions must be made in planning.

There is not one way to plan a unit. A unit plan is a *flexible* guide that should be adjusted as you proceed to meet the needs of your students. No matter how you plan your unit, it is important that you put it in writing. It is in the best interest of all to plan the unit collaboratively with colleagues who teach the same grade/subject.

It should be noted that before you plan a unit, you should have a good handle on what the students already know so that you can connect prior knowledge to the new knowledge to be obtained in the unit. If you have performed a diagnostic evaluation using formal and informal assessments such as pretests, observations, and interviews, this evaluation process will assist you in determining students' prior knowledge. The Student Diagnosis Form as a Guide to Instructional Planning, presented in chapter 3, textbox 3.3, is a tool you can use to perform a comprehensive diagnosis of each student.

Units may be prepared as single topics, integrated with other subjects, or as themes. Though there is no one way to plan a unit, almost all plans have certain elements in common.

General Planning Guidelines

In order to plan (and deliver) a unit most effectively, Brooks and Brooks (1999) have proposed some general guiding principles upon which you should concentrate based on current teaching practices: ascertain what knowledge the student already has mastered; present an overview of the unit content introducing large concepts before smaller ones; encourage student participation in planning the unit by seeking and incorporating their questions and goals; whenever possible, use primary sources and hands-on learning experiences as opposed to worksheets and textbooks; assess continuously; have students experience learning largely in groups instead of having the teacher present information most of the time; provide experiences that allow for students to discover knowledge and produce their own theories; and interact with students as a facilitator of knowledge instead of as a conveyor of information.

Unit Components

1. Learning standard(s). Identify which learning standards (Common Core State Standards [CCSS], state, or local) or standard combinations your unit will address. When you plan all units for the academic year, you should aim cover all (or most) standards for that grade level and *all sections of the standards*. This means that all skills embedded in the standards must be addressed.

For example, in the standard, RL. 6.4, "Determine the meaning of words and phrases as they are used in the text, including figurative and connotative meanings; analyze the impact of a specific word choice on meaning and tone," the teacher must cover determining the meaning of words and phrases *as well as* analyzing the impact of a specific word choice.

In the standard, RL.4.2, "Determine the theme of a story, drama, or poem from details in the text; summarize the text," the teacher must cover determining the theme of a text *as well as* summarizing the text.

"Working with only some of (or part of) the standards would make it quite easy to disregard the ones that you don't like, are difficult to teach, or that fall outside your comfort zone" (Lalor, 2016, p. 53.). Also, specificity with respect to listing standards and their parts is a critical guide for the selection of instructional activities to achieve the standard.

Addressing all standards and all parts of the standards will be easier to accomplish if units are prepared collaboratively with colleagues involved in the same grade level or subject area. This collaboration will also facilitate placing foundational skills early in the academic year, the proper progression of the standards, and opportunities to practice complex skills.

(It must be mentioned that Marzano [2017] has reported that even though standards have been around for a long time, and one would think by now fine-tuned in all subjects and grades, it would take 15,000 hours to teach all the K-12 standards with only 9,000 hours available to do so, a situation that still persists. Marzano suggests that this problem can be resolved if proficiency scales [chapter 3] that focus on important content are created.)

2. Topic/theme. This part includes the unit title. It should be narrow enough to give the unit a focus. "Weapons" and "Medical Discoveries" are unit titles that are too broad. Also, if the title is presented as a question, this format will tend to capture the interest of the students. For example, the above broad unit titles can be narrowed down and changed to questions such as, "How has weaponry changed throughout the ages?" and "How have recent medical discoveries influenced the average life span?"

3. Introduction. In this section make sure it is clear in your own mind and then put in writing the overall nature and scope of the topic or theme to be taught, considering the grade and learners.

Identify the organizing (big) ideas and essential questions that the unit will address. Essential questions serve as an umbrella for the unit. Therefore, activities, assignments, and assessments should be designed to assist students in answering the essential questions. The questions should be arguable, relevant to students' lives, and student-friendly. Essential questions should focus on deeper meaning, not the type answerable in a word or sentence.

Some examples of essential questions are: How does what we eat affect our health? How did the culture of the North and South contribute to the causes of the Civil War?

Nonexamples of essential questions are: Which foods contain calcium? What battles did the Union win?

Allot just enough time to cover the applicable content. In order to make your instruction appropriate to the developmental level of the student, remember the general rule that very young children's units should be relatively short, approximately one week, with increasing numbers of weeks as students proceed through upper elementary and middle school grades to approximately six weeks for high school students.

With the reality of time constrictions in mind, identify the major skills, concepts, problems, and issues that will be covered. Explain the importance of the unit, why it should be studied, what relevance it has to the students, and how you will communicate that relevance.

Plan one or two initial activities to stimulate interest and questions.

If developmentally appropriate for your students, it would be beneficial for you in the unit introduction to apply the first two parts of the popular four-part KWLH strategy used to guide student inquiry.

K stands for, "What do I already Know about this subject?"
W asks, "What do I Want to know?"
L represents, "What did I Learn?"
H stands for, "How I can learn more?"

Have the students involved personally by writing answers to the questions, "What do I already Know?" and "What do I Want to know?" This information can be part of your diagnostic assessment because the information is valuable in assisting you in deciding if parts of the content you originally planned to cover should be modified. The last two parts of KWLH, "What did I Learn?" and "How I can learn more?" can be determined after instruction.

Proficiency scales (chapter 3) can be distributed with students determining what they already know.

4. Content outline. The first step, and perhaps the most difficult at this point, is determining essential from supplemental content (Marzano, 2003). You cannot teach it all. After you have decided on the essential content and essential questions, the content outline serves as a general guideline regarding the sequence of instruction. Narrow the thoughts you wrote in the introduction by writing in outline form what the students will learn in terms of topics, subtopics, concepts, issues, problems, and skills. Given the general timeframe you have indicated, assign an approximate time you will allot for each topic, question, and concept identified.

Whenever possible, *obtain student input regarding content.* For example, if you are preparing a unit on the culture of a particular group, ask the students if there is anything in particular that they would like to learn about that group. Student input will be easier if you have used initiating activities introducing the unit to stimulate questions.

Have a list of key terms the students should know, preferably in order of introduction. These terms should be displayed. But unless you are teaching vocabulary *per se* as part of your unit, your focus should be on activities, not on vocabulary development.

Always take advantage of current events that can be used to make more relevant connections to your content and instruction. For instance, if there is to be an important election, tie this event to a unit on Elections. If there has been a recent earthquake, tsunami, hurricane, tornado, or volcanic eruption, incorporate the economic impact of these events into a unit on economics or have the students study the causes of earthquakes, tsunamis, hurricanes, tornadoes, or volcanoes in a science unit.

A valuable part of planning the content outline is determining a content organizer for the students. This organizer may be an advance organizer, where the content is presented in a written hierarchy of concepts, or a graphic organizer such as a concept map where the content is represented visually (Ewy, 2003; Hyerle, 1996, 2004).

5. Goals. Goals are achieved over the long term and are the results the students should accomplish by the time the unit is completed.

Goals should lead not to just knowledge but deeper understanding. Wiggins and McTighe (2011) have indicated that this type of understanding is demonstrated by the students' ability "to *explain, interpret, apply, shift perspective, empathize,* and *self-assess*" (p. 4, italics in the original). When goals reflect these attributes, a high level of corresponding authentic performance (chapter 3) can then be designed to indicate student achievement at these levels.

Goals clearly offer direction and overall thrust to the unit. Once developed, the goals should be communicated explicitly to the students along with the reasons why the goals are important, how they can be applied in the real world, and how they will affect the students *personally*.

Unless goals (and subsequently, the objectives) are conveyed to the students, they may not achieve the knowledge the teacher intended, even if the activities that develop the goals are stimulating (Nuthall, 1999). The previous sentence is so critical that you should stop and reread it. It is necessary not only to inform students of goals but also to convey high expectations that the goals will be achieved. This expectation level refers to high achievers and low achievers as well.

Some teachers advocate presenting goals and their importance to the students in writing. This process can be facilitated by distributing proficiency scales to students, discussing the scales, and posting them. Teachers can then keep reminding students of the goals by referring to the posted proficiency scales as the unit progresses.

Students should be asked to prepare a journal (log) where they will record your goals for them and *put in writing their own personal goals* relative to the unit. "I want to understand the root causes of terrorism," "I want to learn about the Israeli-Palestinian conflict," or "I want to understand my own feelings about the results of this election" are examples of personal goals.

Students can then monitor their own work by periodically referring to your goals and theirs to assess progress and to decide if a change in behavior (yours and/or theirs) will better achieve the goals. When you select goals, it is important that they be challenging for all students (Marzano, 2003).

Be aware of the fact that in today's diverse classrooms, one student's challenge is another's boredom. If you have performed the prerequisite assessments (observations, interviews, pretests) to make a diagnostic assessment, you will be in a better position to know what the students already know and, therefore, which goals will be challenging.

Goals are extremely important in any organization (Covey, 2004). Though he promoted his ideas for the success of the industrial community, he deemed them applicable also in education. Covey proposed several situations relevant to schools regarding goals. They should be clear to all, measurable, and planned together and have corresponding assessments.

All students and the teacher should hold each class member accountable for achieving goals. And most important, there must be a positive, safe, and supportive classroom environment in which students feel valued and thereby willing to work on achieving goals (adapted from Covey, 2004, pp. 370–71).

Many teachers find it useful to turn goals, just as unit titles, into questions that are subsequently exhibited in the classroom.

When all class members function in cooperation with each other and support each other, there is a high probability that all will achieve the goals. The teachers should foster this type of cooperation.

To increase the chances that students will achieve the goals, scoring rubrics (chapter 3) should be designed with students, when appropriate, for each teacher and student goal as soon as the goals are established (Marzano, 2007). Scoring rubrics known to students in advance of instruction not only remind students of what they should achieve but also allow students to self-assess along the way.

In addition to rubrics, proficiency scales (chapter 3) can perform a major role in informing students explicitly what progress they have made in achieving goals and where the students still have to go. Remember that proficiency scales should be developed with several teachers working districtwide after selecting standards, unpacking them, and determining essential content.

6. Objectives. The goals you identified must be further broken down into objectives. Objectives are frequently referred to interchangeably in curriculum literature as behavioral objectives, instructional objectives, or performance objectives. (Those that are referred to as educational objectives are often actually goals because, even though they include the word

"objective," educational objectives are achievable over a longer period of time.)

Keep in mind that goals are stated in broad terms, and express what the students should accomplish by the end of the unit. Objectives derive their content from goals. As opposed to goals, objectives are achievable over a shorter period of time, usually at the end of a lesson, and are expressed more specifically.

Objectives are written to communicate clearly to students what they are expected to achieve. This communication is particularly important, because as indicated in principles of learning verified by brain research (chapter 3), students who are aware of objectives are more likely to achieve them.

Objectives should describe explicitly what the student will be able to do as a result of instruction. The performance should be expressed as an observable verb that is clear enough so that several people viewing the student would be able to agree that the performance has actually taken place.

Some examples of observable verbs are state, recite, define, explain, evaluate, compare, identify, analyze, and demonstrate (depending upon what follows).

Some nonexamples of observable verbs are see, know, understand (demonstrate the understanding or knowledge of which essentially means understand or know), grasp the meaning of, learn, believe, and appreciate. While these nonexamples are acceptable when writing goals, which are general statements achievable over the long term, these are not acceptable when writing specific objectives, which are achievable over the short term (the lesson).

It is also important to distinguish between verbs used as activities and verbs used as objectives (results). "Cut" different shapes and superimpose them on a template (an instructional activity): it can lead to "identify" shapes (an objective/result). "Pour" water from a quart pitcher into as many cups as possible (an instructional activity): it can lead to "state" how many cups equal one quart (an objective/result).

The objectives should cover several levels of the cognitive, affective, and psychomotor domains. The purpose of including the three domains is not to have every level of each domain represented but to ensure challenge and variety for all your students. It cannot be overemphasized that you communicate the objectives of each lesson and that the students know the objectives. For the purpose of this review, table 4.1 provides a list of cognitive, affective, and psychomotor objectives to guide you in offering a variety of challenges for your students.

There are other taxonomies that can be used to help design learning objectives. The Structure of Observed Learning Outcome (SOLO) is a model describing five levels of increasing complexity in a student's understanding

Table 4.1. A Summary of the Domains

Levels	Task	Corresponding verbs
Cognitive		
Knowledge	Recall basic information or specific facts; remember terms, principles, theories	State, define, identify, list, recognize, recite, outline, name, select
Comprehension	Take basic information and translate, interpret, or describe it in student's own words	Compare, summarize, describe, generalize, restate, rewrite, give an example, demonstrate, estimate
Application	Transfer new information to a new situation	Manipulate, modify, use, relate, demonstrate, predict, apply, perform, solve
Analysis	Break information into its component parts	Arrange, distinguish between, discriminate, differentiate, classify, separate
Synthesis	Put information together in new ways	Devise, construct, assemble, generate, predict, rearrange
Evaluation	Make informed opinions, judgments, and decisions based on clear criteria	Interpret, rate, evaluate, support, appraise, defend
Affective		
Receiving	Willingness of a student to attend to a particular event, stimulus, or phenomenon suggested by another without coercion	Demonstrates, listens, selects, chooses, gives
Responding	Demonstrates behavior that responds voluntarily to the original event, stimulus, or phenomenon	Assists, discusses, reads, performs, selects, chooses
Valuing	Accepts beliefs and values Argues, justifies, invites, joins, protests, supports	Argues, justifies, invites, joins, protests, supports
Organization	Builds a personal value system	Defends, integrates, adheres, prepares, relates, explains
Characterization	Behaves consistently with his/her beliefs and values	Revises, performs, influences, verifies, displays
Psychomotor		
Movement	Display of gross motor coordination	Walk, run, jump, carry, lift, grasp
Manipulation	Display of fine motor coordination	Tune, turn, adjust, assemble, thread, paste, build
Communication	Express feelings and ideas	Draw, explain, write, describe
Creation	Integrate achievement in all domains	Perform, design, create, invent, choreograph

of content (Biggs & Collis, 1982). SOLO provides teachers and students the opportunity to deepen learning of subjects, as well as assess their achievement as they proceed through the learning experience. The SOLO levels of understanding are:

Prestructural. The student shows a lack of understanding of content and uses too simple a way of going about a task.

Unistructural. The student responds by focusing only on one relevant point.

Multistructural. The student responds by focusing on several points, but they are not integrated.

Relational. The student integrates several aspects of a task into a coherent whole.

Extended-abstract. The student conceptualizes the coherent whole into a higher abstraction level and transfers or generalizes this abstraction level to a new content area.

Another taxonomy tool is the Webb Depth of Knowledge (DOK) levels (Webb, Alt, Ely, & Vesperman, 2005). Its purpose is to help teachers create rich environments in which students are exposed to learning at high levels. This exposure is particularly important now that standards are designed to promote more rigor.

The Webb DOK organizes tasks with respect to the thinking complexity necessary to complete them successfully. The DOK levels are:

Level 1—Recall and reproduction. Tasks involve recalling facts and rote application of simple procedures. Some verbs at this level include list, identify, label, quote, arrange, match, define, and state.

Level 2—Skills and concepts. Students decide on an approach to a task using more than one mental step. Possible verbs at this level include estimate, compare, relate, summarize, categorize, identify patterns, predict, and interpret.

Level 3—Strategic thinking. Thinking becomes more abstract as students use planning and produce evidence. Verbs at this level could include revise, critique, differentiate, assess, formulate, hypothesize, develop a logical argument, or cite evidence.

Level 4—Extended thinking. Students use multiple sources to synthesize information and/or apply knowledge from one domain to solve problems in another. Verbs at this level may include design, critique, create, prove, connect, analyze, or synthesize.

The purpose in using taxonomies and domains is to guide teachers in planning instruction so that students are exposed to varieties of objectives and corresponding activities that lead to varieties of outcomes and offer students the opportunity to use progressively more complex cognitive processes.

Marzano (2017) has recommended a curriculum shift that would emphasize the development of cognitive skills. He offered a scope and sequence of cognitive skills for grade K-8. These skills include generating conclusions, identifying common logical errors, presenting and supporting claims, navigating digital sources, problem solving, decision making, experimenting, investigating, identifying basic relationships between ideas, and generating and manipulating mental images. Teachers must become adept at performing these skills themselves in order to cultivate them in students. Then there must be a concerted effort to include age-appropriate cognitive skills in the curriculum.

7. Assessment/formative evaluation. You have already assessed and made a diagnostic evaluation on the basis of that assessment before or at the beginning of the unit. As you proceed through the unit, it is critical for you to measure your progress and that of the students to decide if any reteaching is necessary. To make this decision, there must be an alignment among classroom assessments of student performance, the curriculum, and actual instruction (Cotton, 2000).

A review of assessment, evaluation, and scoring rubrics was offered in chapter 3. The topic is reviewed again briefly here to ensure continuity of the thought process involved in unit planning and especially to stress the importance of determining the assessments (Step 2) immediately after planning objectives (Step 1) and before instructional decisions are made (Step 3). McTighe and Wiggins (2004) have emphasized the value of this "backward design" in unit construction. Since their approach is being used increasingly in school districts, you should be thoroughly familiar with it.

The backward approach is different from that which has been traditionally employed because once objectives have been written, teachers want to instantly proceed to planning instructional activities to assist the students in achieving the objectives.

However, Wiggins (1998) suggested that teachers would be better off if they learned to think first as assessors instead of teachers. He recommended that immediately after writing an objective, the teacher should put on his/her assessor's hat and ask the question, "What counts as evidence of student learning?" In other words, what would the teacher be looking for to make him/her decide whether or not the students are meeting the objectives?

During this stage, assessment is a continuous collection of feedback received to make a formative assessment to see how the students are performing so that, if necessary, instruction can be adjusted. If the objective is stated clearly, it will give direction to the assessment and then to instruction. For instance, if the objective is that the student will be able to compute the length of a hypotenuse, the teacher must first determine what counts as evidence that the student can do this. Will it be by observing him/her perform calculations, by administering a quiz, by having the student create and solve his/her own triangle problems, or any other appropriate activity?

The teacher has to know whether or not to move on or to reteach the computation in a *different* way. If the objective has to be retaught, what alternatives would be provided? Once the objective and assessment are in place, the teacher is in a better position to decide what instruction will be needed to most likely have the student demonstrate achievement. This task is more clearly accomplished if the objective includes an assessment statement (a condition) as illustrated in table 4.2.

You will recall that assessment can be formal or informal and that data may be determined through procedures such as asking questions, observing students, interviewing them, or by quizzes or tests. During the assessment process, students should be responsible for monitoring their own progress in achieving their own personal goals as well as the teacher's unit goals.

As already mentioned earlier in this chapter, an effective way they can do this is by having the students keep a journal (log) noting their achievement, a journal both they and you can check periodically. Students who are not progressing well should assume responsibility for their own performance by suggesting ways of changing their methodology in order to meet goals (Popham, 2008, 2011).

One valuable way to assess student performance is by analyzing samples of student work (Wiggins, 1996). The teacher may do this independently, with other teachers, and/or set up student teams to examine each other's work. They could ask the questions such as:

"What evidence is there that knowledge has been attained?"
"Where are there persistent errors?"
"Where are there misconceptions?"
"What prerequisite knowledge had not been mastered that allowed misconceptions to occur?"

Table 4.2. Objectives and Corresponding Assessment Statement

Content component of objective	Condition (assessment statement)
Label the parts of a flower	on a drawing of the structure of a flower
Identify an adjective	by distinguishing adjectives from a list of all the parts of speech
Explain the causes of the Civil War	in a set of coherent paragraphs

On the basis of the analysis, all or some of the students can move on, or the content can be retaught in a *different* way for those in need. One of the pervasive criticisms of remedial instruction is that during remediation, students are exposed to the same methodology that was ineffective for them in the first place.

Cotton (2000) has researched validated approaches to reteaching. One of these approaches is "using different materials and strategies for re-teaching than those used for initial instruction, rather than merely providing a 'rehash' of previously taught lessons" (p. 26).

Examining samples of student work in *all* subjects is a productive way to perform diagnostic teaching by analyzing errors and determining understanding as well as misunderstanding. As already recommended, this examination is most effective when it is performed collaboratively with other teachers.

8. Instructional procedures. After making explicit both objectives and methods of assessment, the next decision is selecting the best possible way to teach the objectives so that the student will be able to demonstrate performance on the assessments. You will recall that McTighe and Wiggins (2004) described this process as first identifying the desired results (goals and objectives), then determining what would be acceptable evidence that the goals and objectives have been met, and finally planning the corresponding learning experiences. McTighe and Wiggins (2004) have stated that using this backward design "helps to avoid the twin sins of activity-oriented and coverage-oriented curriculum planning" (p. 25).

There should be a choice of instructional activities provided for students, especially when it comes to independent work.

At this point in the planning process, it would be worthwhile to remind you that merely exposing students to different activities, no matter how exciting and dynamic they are, will not produce their desired results unless *the students know the purpose* of those activities (Nuthall, 1999; Nuthall & Alton-Lee, 1993). It is also worthwhile to caution you not to mistake activity with achievement.

The most important deliberations concerning the selection of overall instructional procedures (teaching strategies) are: "Which would be most suitable to meet the students' cognitive, cultural, and developmental needs, given the objective and its corresponding assessment?" "Will the students need more teacher direction?" "Will some of the students be better off in a student-centered situation?" and "What learning experience choices will be offered?"

Just as students should be involved in suggesting goals and their assessments, students should also be involved in suggesting appropriate instructional procedures for attaining goals and meeting the assessments.

Before continuing, it would be valuable to note, especially when dealing with lower-achieving students, what MIT professor of mathematics and computer science, Seymour Papert, has stated:

> Every maker of video games knows something that the makers of curriculum don't seem to understand. You'll never see a video game being advertised as being easy. Kids who do not like school will tell you it's not because it's too hard. It's because it's—boring.

Keep this in mind when planning the curriculum.

9. Resources and materials. The selection of appropriate corresponding materials is integral to the success of the unit. The materials must match the objectives, assessment, and instruction. When preparing a unit, teachers will frequently list only the textbook. But the textbook is far from the best resource, especially when it is the only resource. Primary sources are much more effective and make the learning experiences more related to the real (authentic) world.

Students must be actively engaged in learning and must use many senses. Resources and materials can be placed into four general categories: technology, manipulatives, printed materials, and the community.

Technology. In many respects, when it comes to technology, students have left teachers behind. Moreover, technology is changing so rapidly that in order to keep up with it, teachers need continuous professional development. Currently, technological resources include camcorders, overhead projectors, TV/VCRs, digital video disk (DVD) players, audio recorders, cameras, computers, mobiles, smartphones, and many other devices that will be new to the market by the time you read this section. Video and audio clips themselves can be extremely useful and stimulating.

Technology, especially computer technology, should be infused into the curriculum. Computer technology is a valuable resource for research, reinforcement, and enrichment. But as with all resources, it should complement and supplement the teacher's role and help tailor information for each learner's needs. *Technology should not be used for the sake of technology but should be used when it will be effective in implementing goals and objectives.*

It is unlikely that anytime soon any technology will replace an outstanding teacher or inspiring professor. Even Bill Gates has acknowledged that technology is just a tool and to get students working together and motivating them, it is the teacher who is most important.

Manipulatives. Models, mockups, fraction pieces, counting sticks, and rocks are some examples of hands-on materials students can work with to provide them with concrete experiences. Games/simulations can also be used effectively to reinforce learning or provide opportunities for discovery.

For example, the game, New Town, provides the opportunity for students to build a completely new town from acquiring the land to constructing homes and deciding what services must be offered and how to organize them. A detailed study indicated that age-old board games have assisted students from low-income families in achieving large, long-lasting gains in math (Cavanagh, 2008).

Lonsdorf (2017) reported on a game, March Mammal Madness, that students play online. In this game, real animals, represented as brackets, conduct fictional battles with students using a lot of science to predict the winner.

Games can also be adapted for specific instructional objectives. Bingo can be adapted to match vocabulary words with definitions or reinforce basic math facts. For instance, if B 6 is called, anyone who has on a Bingo game card space a mathematical computation that equals 6 can cover the space. Examples of some computations that will yield this result are: $6 + 0$; $0 + 6$; $54 \div 9$; $1 + 1 + 1 + 3$; $10 - 4$; 3×2; 2×3; and $7 - 1$. Card games such as War can teach or reinforce equal to, greater than, and less than.

Printed materials. Textbooks have value when they are *not* the sole or major means for teaching content but enrich, reinforce, and clarify meaning. Workbooks and worksheets can provide drill and practice once a concept is already learned, but remember that worksheets do not grow dendrites (Tate, 2003). Newspapers, magazines, anecdotes, and famous quotes can provide timely, as well as relevant, instruction mostly as primary sources.

Catalogs such as the J.C. Penney catalog or other comparable home shopping materials can reinforce math and language arts concepts. Students can create simulated purchases that involve looking up items listed in alphabetical order; determining costs for several items; percentage discounts; shipping weights; and measurements for clothing, carpeting, and completing forms.

Document-based questions (DBQs), generally used as a means for assessment, can also be used for instruction. These documents are motivational because they represent brain-compatible primary sources for learning.

Regarding the use of materials in general, you should remember that if the teacher uses activities and materials that relate to the students' cultural backgrounds, the students respond more favorably.

The community. Unless your school is in an extremely rural community, students will have access to libraries, banks, supermarkets, and other stores. These facilities frequently have important resources for field trips or for displaying authentic performance tasks or products created by students.

To illustrate, a student may come up with a new computer program for tying together several banking services. Students may have completed a nutrition project or a cost-effective shopping guide by comparing shopping lists from several different supermarket flyers. Field trips can be conducted to nurseries as part of studying plants, to the fire department while studying a unit on safety, or to a courthouse while studying law.

Parents are important community members who can offer enrichment and reinforcement. Many teachers have taken advantage of the parents' occupations to provide a different way to learn material, either as a motivating force in the beginning of a unit or as part of a culminating activity at the end. For example, a parent who is a dentist can be invited to demonstrate equipment or techniques that will stimulate curiosity at the beginning of a unit on health or tie together important points at the end. Parents with relevant occupations or interests can also mentor students on unit projects.

Parent involvement may not solely be academic. "[T]he types of relationships and encounters that are in place between teachers and parents can have a profound effect on student learning and growth (with) countless student transformations after reaching out to their families" (Mbadu, 2008).

Guest speakers whose services are connected to a unit of study can also be invited to the class. As with parents, it is necessary for the teacher to inform the guest speaker about the knowledge and developmental background of the students so that the presentation is appropriate both cognitively and content-wise for the students. After the initial presentation by the guest speaker, students can be engaged in follow-up questioning and possibly in pursuing more interaction and field experiences with the guest speaker.

It is imperative that materials and activities be previewed to ensure that they are appropriate for students' cognitive and developmental levels, match objectives, and are *not activities for the sake of activities*. Materials should be cost-effective, simple to use, and, when feasible, brought to class by students. Which student would not be excited about seeing *his/her* cuddly toy, magazine, or model of a derrick being used by the teacher for instruction in the class? Remember that in accessing materials, you do not necessarily have to be creative, but you can be resourceful.

10. Correlations with other curriculum areas. Whether you are preparing a topic unit, or working on an integrated or thematic unit, it is productive for the contextual learning of your students to give some thought regarding how the content of your unit and other subjects are interrelated. Even though some of these correlations may be obvious to you, they may not become obvious to your students unless you consciously plan to make connections for them.

For example, studying "Methods of Warfare" is more closely related to science, history, and economics but can also include language arts, the arts, or mathematics. Language arts activities for this unit could incorporate keeping

diaries; writing letters of invitation to class activities, letters requesting information on the unit, or thank-you letters to resource people; writing a play; or
writing a newsletter.

Arts activities might incorporate organizing exhibits; constructing models
of weapons; making overheads, slides, or videos; creating diagrams, charts,
and maps; designing costumes or sets; writing war songs; painting murals; or
constructing timelines.

Mathematics activities could comprise measuring and purchasing materials
for weapon or costume construction; computing word problems for distance,
angle of projection, speed, or time; constructing a compass; and determining
longitude and latitude of sea targets.

11. Summative assessment/evaluation. At the end of the unit, assessments
    are collected to make a summative assessment evaluating how well the
    students have achieved the unit objectives. Obviously, at the end it is too
    late to make changes, which is why formative assessment is so important.
    The summative evaluation should be flexible by including a variety of
    methods and choices for demonstrating mastery.

Performance tasks and products, projects, portfolios, and a final teacher-
made test (chapter 3) can be used to evaluate students. Performance tasks
and products should be designed to be important, high-level, and authentic
(something a student would have to confront in the world outside of school)
and should demonstrate the achievement of not one but *all* the unit goals.

Scoring rubrics should be constructed (with students, when possible) to
provide an objective method of determining student accomplishments. "Share
the culminating performance tasks and accompanying rubric(s) so students
will know what will be expected and how their work will be judged (and)
show models of student work on similar tasks so students can see what quality work looks like" (Tomlinson & McTighe, 2006, p. 88).

During the summative evaluation, classes that used KWLH in the beginning of the unit to decide what they already Know and Would like to know
can now describe the L part, what they have Learned, and the H part, How
they can find out more.

In addition to KWLH, a significant activity in the evaluation process is
having students reflect on the new information they have acquired in the unit,
how this information can be integrated into what they previously learned, and
how they can *adjust* their knowledge accordingly. The students should put
this information in writing.

As already indicated repeatedly in your prior reading, depending on their
stage of development, it is an effective practice to have students participate in

Table 4.3. Best Practices for Unit Planning (T for Implementation)

Criteria (descriptors)	Performance indicators (examples)
Before planning the unit, the teacher reviewed the Best Practices for Implementing (Brain-Compatible) Learning Theory OI collaborated with colleagues to plan the unit	
Introduction The teacher performed a diagnosis of the students' prior knowledge identified the learning standard(s) on which the content is based selected a topic/theme narrow enough to give the unit a focus described the nature and scope of the unit listed big ideas identified major (essential) questions and content selected (collaboratively districtwide prepared) proficiency scales for essential content indicated the relation of the unit to learners' lives capitalized on learners' interests introduced a stimulating initiating activity	
Content outline listed topics and subtopics indicated an approximate time frame for each topic and subtopic prepared, displayed, and discussed an organizer (verbal/visual) for the content	
Goals flowed logically from the CCSSs or other local or state standard reflected deep understanding included those suggested by students communicated clearly and displayed in classroom presented so that responsibility of class members to support each other and hold each other responsible for achieving goals was clear offered corresponding scoring rubrics developed with students, when appropriate	
Objectives (performance, behavioral, instructional) wrote objectives correctly (observable, student oriented, results of instruction) and included an assessment statement covered several domains and domain levels led collectively to goal(s) planned objectives that included the development of age-appropriate complex cognitive skills	
Formative assessment matched objectives guided teacher instruction	

(Continued)

Table 4.3.   (Continued)

Criteria (descriptors)	Performance indicators (examples)
provided proficiency scales to students to assess what explicit knowledge/skills were mastered and where improvement was needed	
allowed periodically for student self-assessment of goals and self-adjustment of learning tactics	
Instructional procedures	
matched formative assessments	
provided for the uniqueness of all learners (genders, interests, cultural differences, cognitive and developmental levels)	
offered a variety of activities (field trip[s], simulations, technology, educational games, guest speakers, discussion groups, panels, committee work, role-playing, drama, etc.)	
incorporated students' suggestions	
used mainly hands-on activities	
Instructional materials	
used materials that were meaningful to the students	
incorporated largely primary sources	
demonstrated creativity and/or resourcefulness	
used materials that appealed to many senses	
Summative assessment (evaluation)	
employed high-level performance tasks and/or products that demonstrated achievement of all goals	
offered corresponding scoring rubric(s) for performance tasks and/or products	
offered students choices	
included teacher self-evaluation and input from students	
requested that students put in writing how the information they received in the unit related to prior relevant information and how they adjusted their knowledge accordingly	
final paper and pencil test included all unit objectives reflecting time allotted to each	
reflected appropriate test construction practices for short answer and essay questions	
if a topic unit was used,	
connected concepts and activities with other curriculum areas	
discussed with colleagues if any changes (modifications, additions, deletions) were needed in the above criteria as a result of new research	

constructing tests and scoring rubrics. Students should have the scoring rubric *before* they embark on any project or task because the rubric is an important teaching, as well as evaluative, tool. And students should be offered the opportunity to choose activities for both instruction and evaluation.

As previously indicated, students should also have access to any knowledge and/or skill proficiency scales relevant to the unit to keep aware of their knowledge/skill acquisition.

A most integral part of the evaluation process that must be reiterated is self-reflection on the part of the teacher. Even though assessment may have been continuous throughout the unit, s/he should consider at the end of the unit what was positive, what did not go well, and how the unit planning and/or its implementation could have been improved. A critical component in gathering this information is securing *input from the students*.

The Best Practices for Unit Planning OI, table 4.3, provides the criteria to plan successful units. Note that it is coded T. As you progress, complete the Performance Indicators.

Chapter 5

Proficient Lesson Planning

REVIEW AND UPDATE

This chapter will review how to plan effective and thorough daily lessons. A lesson should develop one or several related objectives listed in the unit (chapter 4).

A carefully thought-out lesson plan actually becomes a *learning* plan that increases teacher productivity and is the best way to meet the needs of all learners (Scherer, 2016). This thought process must become a habit of mind. Just as there is not one way to plan a unit, there is not one way to plan a lesson.

Though it is not realistic or necessary that you implement all parts of the lesson plan outline all of the time (M. Hunter, 1984), you must be aware that frequently omitting parts represents a lost opportunity for your students to learn. A commonly stated rule is that you should conduct each lesson as though you were being observed by your district's superintendent or your school principal.

As in the unit plan, you should put your lesson plan in writing to ensure that you have considered important elements and questions *before* the actual instruction takes place. This process will enhance the probability for student (and your attendant) success.

When planning any instruction, units, or lessons, always check to ensure that you are implementing as many learning principles as possible (see table 2.2).

Lesson Plan Components

The lesson plan components that follow are based on the work of M. Hunter (1982) updated by her associate (R. Hunter, 2004) to include more current research (Marzano, 2017). You should be aware of the fact that even though Madeline Hunter's work has been considered a 20th-century relic, her model has been reaffirmed by recent brain research (Wolfe, 2011). Researcher Mike Schmoker (2011) has indicated that Hunter's planning model is the key to ensuring that all students learn necessary content and intellectual skills. He asserts that Hunter's basic model, in addition to other essential educational practices, can close the achievement gap in five years or fewer.

Hunter's model involves mainly direct instruction, which the research has constantly proved to be superior to inquiry-based instruction (Ellis, 2001; Marzano, 2011). While summarizing the research on Direct Instruction in one of his chapters, Ellis stated:

> It is difficult to know how to conclude a chapter devoted to a topic that has such a solid record of supportive evidence behind it but which is not particularly liked by large numbers of teachers.
>
> Such is the case with Direct Instruction. Well, broccoli has a pretty solid record, and yet it is easy to find people who don't like and won't eat the green stuff. . . . Maybe Direct Instruction is the broccoli of educational practice, good for you but not everybody's favorite dish. (pp. 226–27)

In the past, direct instruction became associated with teacher-dominated lessons and lectures, with students as passive receptors. But direct instruction can be modified to include more active learning and student involvement. Marzano (2017) stresses that regardless of the type of lesson the teacher wants to present, "direct instruction is essential when teachers present new content to students" (p. 29). After this initial content is delivered, many different interactive strategies that engage the students in processing the new content can be employed. The lesson then shifts from teacher direction to student active involvement with a partner or in a group/team to ensure that new information is learned and then reinforced. A shorter time is spent on teacher delivery with a majority of time spent on student involvement, with teacher supervising the access of new information.

1. Analytic diagnosis and description of learners. Planning should be geared to your knowledge of the students. There must be constant purposeful and systematic planning in order to meet the needs of the varieties of students in your classroom, even if it reflects a homogeneous classroom or group.

Though much more information about students comes as you teach, you should, at the very least when you begin working with them, have some understanding of each student's strengths and weaknesses. When you planned your unit, you should have gathered pertinent information by performing a diagnostic evaluation for each student (chapter 3, textbox 3.3). What is his/ her cognitive level of functioning? What knowledge does the student already possess? How may gender affect learning? What attitudes and other affective considerations should you take into account? Are there some student interests you could exploit? What psychomotor needs does the student have? Are there students with exceptionalities, including gifted exceptionalities? What different cultures are represented? Are any of the students non-English speaking? Unless you have a firm handle on each student, you will not know how to competently tailor and assess instructional needs.

2. Learning standard. List the particular learning standard addressed in the lesson. This standard should be one identified in your unit.
3. Goal. State the content or process goal based on your unit. Remember that the goal is a broad statement that will be achieved over the long term, not by the end of the lesson.

Goals do not have to be stated in behavioral (instructional, performance) terms. It cannot be overemphasized that students should be made aware of goals when you introduce the unit. The goal in the lesson should flow from your unit, and, when appropriate, some of the goals should be those of the students. An effective practice is that of reminding students of the particular goal they will be working toward in the lesson and what connection the goal has to their lives.

4. Objective(s). The objective is determined from the goal and answers the question, "What will the students be able to *do* at the end of the lesson that will be *one step* toward demonstrating knowledge of the goal?" The objective should be written in behavioral (instructional, performance) terms and should reflect the lesson topic. The objective can be one identified in the relevant proficiency scale.

Here again, as with the goal, you should inform students the reason for learning the objective and how it is connected to their lives and to the world outside of the classroom. More than one objective may be selected if they are closely related and realistically achievable within the time frame for the lesson.
Example of a goal and one objective that will lead to the goal:

Goal. Create costumes for the class play. (Note that this goal cannot be accomplished within the lesson but over the long term.)
Objective. Given a pattern, the student will be able to cut fabric according to the pattern (one objective achievable within a class period that will lead to the goal).

The objective is of particular importance in lesson planning. It will guide you in identifying the prerequisite knowledge (entry skills) your students need to learn the new content, focus your teaching on the observable results that you will use to validate the acquisition of that new learning (formative assessment), and direct you in deciding what instruction will best facilitate that learning. Even more important, sharing the objective with students will assist them in self-assessment FOR learning (Stiggins, 2007).

5. Entry skills. The lesson you offer must be in context. You want to be aware of what the students can already do so that they will have a scaffold for the lesson. Listing their prerequisite skills in behavioral terms can help you be more accurate in determining what the students already know and can do. (Sometimes an experience like a field trip or a video will be sufficient for you to build a lesson.)

The basic consideration is what experiential *readiness*, prior knowledge, or skills the students have so that they can absorb the objective of the lesson into schema (cognitive structures) already present. It is a frustrating experience and inefficient for the teacher and the student when a lesson does not build on prior knowledge. Some (or all) students may be lost and confused. The teacher then has to go back and teach (or reteach) the prior knowledge before continuing with the planned objective.

Being aware of the prior knowledge of students will also assist you in deciding how much content (chunking) you will be able to deliver.

6. Anticipatory set. Your students must be ready, willing, and able to receive the lesson (Ryan, Cooper, & Tauer, 2008). As already stated, students must be prepared with prerequisite knowledge and/or experience that will serve as a foundation for the lesson. Since they are constantly being bombarded with competing stimuli, students will select those that are interesting and stay with those that are enjoyable.

You will recall that according to brain research, there is no learning without memory and that memory depends on attention (Jensen, 1998). So how do you get that attention? During the anticipatory set, you make students aware of and hooked into the objective. It is your opportunity to stimulate the students' curiosity.

Brain research tells us that the brain can be primed, and if the students know (are primed with) the objective, the chances are that they will achieve it. And since the brain is always paying attention to something, the anticipatory set is your opportunity to concentrate the students' attention on the lesson by thwarting competing stimuli.

The anticipatory set provides *motivation* for gaining this attention. As you already read in chapter 2, motivation should introduce enough frustration to make the students want to go back into equilibrium, and the "going back into equilibrium" involves learning. "Significant learning is frequently accompanied or impelled by discomfort" (Joyce, Weil, & Calhoun, 2004).

Students should be informed regarding why the objective is important and what it means to them personally. Assuming that the students can read, many teachers find that once the objective is elicited, an effective practice is writing it on the board or on a poster. If you are using proficiency scales, and have posted them, you can point to which content indicated on the relevant scale will be addressed in the lesson.

Displaying the objective helps keep the students focused on where they are heading and provides a link to eventually closing the lesson. In addition, as already mentioned, knowing the objective assists students in self-assessing.

Some teachers find it helpful to write the objective in the form of a question. "To calculate the area of a circle" would then become, "How can we calculate the area of a circle?" At the end of the lesson, the students would then decide whether or not they could actually perform the task.

It is also important for you to know whether or not the students are aware of the objective. Just because you state it or one or more of the students can state the objective does not mean that everyone is aware of it. You will have a better handle on knowing how aware the students are of the objective if you have several students repeat the objective not in parrot form but *in their own words*.

Example:

Teacher: How many of you brought your lunch to school?

(All hands go up.) What did you bring? Tom.

Tom: Peanut butter and jelly.

Teacher: (The teacher pats his belly.) One of my favorites. What about you, Henrietta?

Henrietta: A tuna fish sandwich.

(Some members of the class hold their noses, snicker, or say, "Yuk." The teacher ignores the behavior.)

Teacher: Tuna is very good source of protein, Henrietta. Whoever prepared that lunch is smart and must really care about you. And what do you have for lunch, George?

George: A ham sandwich.

Teacher: Also a great source of protein. Well, class, I brought my lunch today, too. (Teacher places his lunch box on the desk.) What do you think is in my lunch box? Frank?

Frank: Soup and crackers.

Teacher: Maybe. What do you think, Johnny?

Johnny: A big Mac.

Teacher: It's possible. And you, Sheila?

Sheila. Chicken nuggets . . . or a hot dog. But . . . but then the hot dog would be cold. (The class laughs.)

Teacher: Good guesses, but in my lunch box is *another* lunch box.

(The students all look at each other with puzzled faces [discomfort level], obviously having been thrown off-balance. The teacher opens his lunch box. The students look with anticipation. In the lunch box is a lima bean. The teacher places the lima bean on his desk.) So what do you think we are going to learn today? (There is a long pause as the teacher observes the still-crinkled faces.) Debbie?

Debbie: How . . . how or why a lima bean is a lunch box?

Teacher: Excellent, Debbie. Now who can say that in another way? Jerry?

Jerry: How a lunch box and a lima bean are the same?

Teacher: Great, Jerry. Give us another way of saying this. Paul?

Paul: What makes a lima bean like lunch?

Note that in the example the teacher did not tell the students at the beginning what the objective of the lesson was. *The objective flowed from the anticipatory set*—what the teacher did to stimulate curiosity so that the students would want to learn the objective: how the lunch box and lima bean were alike.

Some teachers just state the objective at the beginning. For example, a teacher might say, "Today we're going to learn about the parts of a lima bean" or, given a different lesson, "Today we are going to learn how sounds are produced." Merely stating the purpose of the lesson is *much less efficient* than throwing the students a little off-balance in the beginning with the anticipatory set and letting the objective derive from that set.

Another way to get student attention is by introducing a problem whose solution is made possible only by the achievement of the lesson objective. In this type of situation, the learning becomes more meaningful because there is a *reason* to learn something (R. Hunter, 2004).

Example:

> Teacher: "Mrs. Shiller just informed me that our class mothers raised $476 in our cake sale to buy a carpet for our classroom. But before we can buy that carpet, we first have to decide how much we need to cover the floor. And to do this we have to learn how to measure area." Unless the students can measure area (solve the problem by achieving the lesson objective), the class cannot buy the carpet (the reason for the learning).

Time spent on the anticipatory set should be relatively short, leaving the largest portion of lesson time to accomplishing the objective.

6A. Sequence of objectives. At this point the students should be curious to find the answer to the question raised in the anticipatory set and thus achieve the objective. For you to decide what step is next in determining the assessment and instructional process, and, therefore, how you will continue with the lesson, you have to analyze the lesson objective to determine *if* sequence is important. If it is, you have to break up the lesson objective into smaller objectives that will lead to it. Even if sequence is not important, you have to decide which objectives will collectively lead to the lesson objective.

Example: Lesson Objective—The Student Will Be Able to Describe the Digestive Process

That is what the students will do at the *end* of the lesson. How do you get to that final stage? There are intervening steps, a sequence of smaller objectives, also written in behavioral terms, that will lead the students to describing the digestive process. You have to arrange the content so that it makes sense to the learner. Analyzing the sequence of objectives will also help you decide how much absorbable information (chunks) the students will be able to digest. (Pardon the pun.)

In the lesson, new material is delivered into the students' working memory (chapter 2), which is limited. So you must be aware of how much new information (chunks) that memory can hold.

In order for students to be able to describe the digestive process, they have to be able to:

1. explain the function of digestion;
2. identify the organs in the digestive system;
3. locate the organs in the digestive system;
4. describe the function of each organ; and
5. trace different food particles through the digestive system.

When you read these five objectives, you will note that they sequentially and collectively describe the digestive process—the lesson objective. A student who cannot identify the organs will not be able to describe their function. A student who cannot locate the organs will not be able to trace food through them.

Writing these smaller intermittent objectives is often a difficult process for teachers. It takes practice. But the identification of these objectives tells you where to begin after the anticipatory set, with an assessment and an input (instructional) activity that will, as in the example earlier, assist the students in being able to explain the function of digestion.

Identification of smaller intermittent objectives will help you decide how much information (chunks) you can deliver, the best way to deliver it, and what students can do immediately after each chunk to assure attainment of the information/skill. What activities will take the information/skill from working memory into permanent memory? How can the new content be encoded linguistically or nonlinguistically through pictographs, diagrams, charts, or graphic organizers (Marzano, 2007)? How will the new information be summarized with a partner or group?

In addition, identifying intermittent objectives will help you assess the attainment of these objectives as the students proceed and, therefore, whether or not you or they need to adjust instruction along the way. Also, having a clear idea of the sequence of instruction, when sequence is necessary, avoids the problem of sometimes "losing" the students when a critical step in the learning process is omitted.

6B. Assessment of objectives. It is the instinct of teachers, once they determine objectives, to "teach" by immediately delving into ways of achieving them. After all, "teaching" is the goal for which teachers were educated. But it has long been a criticism that too much education is concerned with input, not results.

Often teachers (and students) are constantly "doing things," but the students are not learning. This situation is similar to the police department's implementing different policies to fight crime after which the crime rate is still high. You must keep your eye on the target—student learning. Decide first how you will assess each intermittent objective to assist you in knowing whether or not instruction should continue or whether or not you have to take a different track (Wiggins & McTighe, 2005).

Using again the previous digestion example, you should decide for *each* intermittent objective how you will know whether or not the students are "getting it." Students might explain the function of digestion by simply restating it or by giving an example. They may identify and locate the organs by filling the names of the organs on a diagram. Frequently, the same assessment can cover more than one objective.

What is NOT productive in assessment is asking questions like, "Does everybody understand?" "Do you all agree?" "All right?" or "Okay?" If you really want to know if the students understand, *ask questions about the content.*

Assessment may occur by an informal method such as simple observation, or it may be having the students identify organ parts on a model, draw their own diagram, name the organs on a diagram you provide, place the parts of a model together, or any other assessment that makes sense. You could also use hand signals to assess. "Raise your right hand if the pyloric valve comes before the stomach and your left hand if the pyloric valve comes after." You will note how quickly students signal and which signals are correct and which are incorrect. Students who look at others' hands before raising theirs will indicate uncertainty.

You can offer self-correcting materials for students to use and, when applicable, have peers check each other. Always keep the students involved in and responsible for their own assessment (Stiggins, 2005). Identifying the assessment(s) for the objectives ensures that your students, not you, will be covering the curriculum.

6C. Instructional strategies (learning experiences). In selecting instructional strategies, also referred to as input, there are a myriad of possibilities. This decision becomes more complex given your need to provide instructional options for different student needs.

Before you continue reading, keep in mind that objectives are the *results* of instruction. Once you have decided the main objective, the intermittent objectives that will lead to it, and how each will be assessed, you will be in a better position to decide the most effective learning experiences the students should have in order to meet each assessment.

You will note in table 5.1 that several strategies such as problem solving and discovery are listed in several columns and can cover different learning outcomes. Your challenge here is keeping the students' attention and keeping them meaningfully engaged. "[T]he most effective instruction is that which addresses multiple modalities: instruction where students get to hear, see, touch, and discuss . . . there is no one best way" (R. Hunter, 2004, p. 7).

At this point it is important to remind you that just because students are involved in activities, this does not necessarily mean that the students are achieving. They must be prompted regarding the purpose of the activity and assessed regarding what they have achieved from their involvement in it.

Sometimes each intermittent objective, assessment, and learning experience (input, strategy) needs a one-to-one correspondence. In other cases the same assessment and learning experience can cover several objectives.

As indicated previously, knowledge of your students is particularly crucial in making learning experience decisions. It is now a nationwide trend

Table 5.1. Instructional Strategies and Their Learning Outcomes

Concepts/principles	Skills	Attitudes/social development
Lectures	Drill and practice	Role-playing
Debates	Computer-assisted instruction	Dramas
Panels	Modeling	Cooperative learning
Videos	Demonstrations	Discussions
Guest speakers	Games/simulations	Videos
Discovery	Independent study	Problem solving
Internet research		Games/simulations
Concept attainment		Debates
Concept formation		Case studies
Advance organizers		Discovery
Mastery learning/contracts		
Cooperative learning		
Learning activity centers		
Case studies		
Problem solving		
Demonstrations		
Dramas		
Discussions		
Games/simulations		
Independent study		

to distinguish between accommodations and modifications, two distinctions with a difference (Beech & Barnitt, 2001).

Accommodations are changes in the ways students are taught, the assignments they are eventually given after the lesson, and the way students are assessed/evaluated. When accommodations are necessary, there is *no change* in the objectives covered.

Modifications are actual *changes in the content* (objectives) taught. These may include objectives for partial requirement completions, alternate curriculum goals, and different diplomas. Some of your students may actually need modifications. These students are most frequently those who are *significantly* below age/grade level.

Modifications are those adaptations (changes) that are made to curriculum, instruction, classroom set-up, or assessment. Therefore, they change the instruction level, the course content, and the performance criteria (Castagnera, Fisher, Rodifer, & Sax, 1998).

To summarize, accommodations change *how* instruction is delivered: modifications change *what* is taught.

7. Materials. After you decide what instructional strategies you will use, identify the matching materials you and the students will need. Make sure

the materials are meaningful to the students, are as concrete and multisensory as possible, and engage the students actively in hands-on learning whenever appropriate. Remember that the hands are the most important organ of the brain and that, whenever possible, primary sources should be used (Jensen, 1998).

8. Classroom organization. Will the students be arranged for whole class, small group, individualized instruction, or a combination of these patterns? The selection should be based on students' needs in achieving the objective.

When the teacher is delivering the initial content (chunks), students are arranged for whole class instruction. When ensuring encoding of the initial content and deepening its understanding before continuing with additional content, students are usually arranged to interact in pairs or in small groups.

Countless activities can take place in the interactive groups. These activities could include summarizing the new information, categorizing it, making predictions about the content and what may follow, constructing questions, answering questions, arranging team contests, and highlighting important information, and the list goes on impeded only by the teacher's imagination and resourcefulness (Marzano, 2017).

Brain science tells us that physical movement facilitates the processing of information (Jensen, 1998). Movement is one of the arts (chapter 2) that fosters cognitive, emotional, and psychomotor pathways to the brain. Physical activity increases blood flow to the brain, which in turn increases student energy level and engagement (Marzano & Pickering, 2011). While setting up the groups that will absorb new information, or in delivering the initial information itself, it would be most productive to decide what physical movement (activity) would be appropriate to accompany the processing of this information.

Depending on the students' age, some of these movements could include hand signals, hand raising, standing, stretching, jumping, changing group membership, group relocation, acting out new information, or any other appropriate physical action.

9. Modeling of skills. The teacher ensures that the content or directions presented are clear by providing examples and/or demonstrations. The modeling you select depends on the learning outcome (lesson objective). Does it involve a concept or set of concepts or a skill? Concepts are modeled by providing examples and/or products (samples). When offering examples and products, select those that connect to the students' experiences. Skills are best modeled by demonstrations. For solving a problem or applying a skill (process), you can also model by thinking out loud.

10. Guided practice. During guided practice, the new material is reinforced. If the objective involves movement such as bending a piece of glass, then drill or rote rehearsal is in order. Rote rehearsal involves practicing the material over and over again in the same way.

But since most of school learning involves semantic knowledge, or meaning, elaborative rehearsal is necessary. Elaborative rehearsal involves practicing the material in different ways to strengthen connections and deepen understanding—an expansion of behavior theory through brain research. Moreover, you may recall from chapter 2 that research conducted by Nuthall (1999) concluded that content should be learned in *four differ-ent ways*.

There are many options available for elaborative rehearsal. These include repeating the material in varied ways, teaching the material to someone else, drawing a picture of the content, writing what was learned, working with a partner or group to explain the content and/or discuss applications of the content, playing a game, and applying the objective, to name a few. Always remember that the ways of rehearsing should be personalized.

Grouping is particularly important during guided practice, particularly small groups. The type of group should reflect the *purpose* of the practice. Groups could be involved in peer tutoring, think-pair-share, or cooperative learning. Group activities might include round table, buzz session, or fish bowl. For a fuller discussion of grouping, see Pagliaro (2012).

11. Closure. During closure, the lesson content is tied together. It should be clear in your mind how this will be done. Will it be summarized by the students? Will they explain how the content was personally meaningful? Will the students draw conclusions? Closure is an appropriate time to go back to the displayed objective of the lesson to determine if the students can *perform* the objective. If the objective was displayed in the form of a question, can the students *answer* the question?

Using the same examples of lesson objectives presented earlier in this chapter, students could explain how a lima bean is like a lunch box or describe the digestive process. They could do this orally, write in their journals, or perform any other activity, which demonstrates knowledge of the objective.

12. Independent practice. Remember that most original learning is forgotten within the first 24 hours (chapter 2). Therefore, during independent practice, understanding is deepened further as the teacher provides additional reinforcement, the students do on their own. It may be a homework

Table 5.2. Best Practices for Lesson Planning and Implementation

Criteria (descriptors)	Performance indicators (examples)
Goal listed relevant goal identified in unit	
Objective(s) stated main lesson objective(s) appropriately (observable, outcome based, student oriented) that flowed from the goal	
Entry skills identified students' prior relevant knowledge/ skills in behavioral (performance) terms	
Anticipatory set provided an interesting and engaging hook connected content to prior learning led into lesson objective that was restated by several students *in their own words* The teacher displayed the objective explained how the objective was connected to students' lives connected the objective to one of the scores on the appropriate proficiency scale	
Sequence of objectives listed intermittent objectives (in behavioral terms) that led to the main lesson objective listed objectives in sequential order, when sequence was important delivered objectives in absorbable chunks for working memory identified activities for immediately reinforcing the absorbable chunks implemented physical movement activities to process information	
Assessment expressed assessment clearly for each objective (though one assessment may cover several objectives) asked students to self-assess after reinforcing each identified chunk	
Corresponding instructional strategies matched the sequence of objectives and assessment employed several senses involved students with hands-on activities provided differentiated options	

(Continued)

Table 5.2.   (Continued)

Criteria (descriptors)	Performance indicators (examples)

Materials
used materials that included multisensory
   experiences
selected materials connected to students'
   lives
included mainly primary sources, whenever
   possible

Classroom organization
selected student arrangements that would
   most appropriately reinforce each
   absorbable amount of information/skill
   delivered

Modeling
The teacher demonstrated the skills (if the
   objective was a skill)
provided examples or products (if the
   objective was a concept or set of concepts)

Guided practice
involved students in elaborative rehearsal by
   reinforcing the objective in several *different*
   ways

Closure
asked the students to *perform* the objective

Independent practice
provided activities that were meaningful to
   and engaging for students

Evaluation of learning
measured the attainment of the lesson
   objective for each student

Follow-up lesson
communicated next lesson to class
discussed with colleagues if any changes
   (modifications, additions, deletions) were
   needed in the previous criteria as a result
   of new research

assignment, constructing a different diagram from one used in the lesson, arranging the content in a different way, or practicing on worksheets. It cannot be overemphasized that homework, just as any other assignment or activity, should be *meaningful* work, not busy work.

After content is learned through direct instruction, and reinforced and deepened through elaborative rehearsal, independent practice offers a significant opportunity for students to *apply* what they have learned.

13. Evaluation of learning. What will each learner do at the end of the lesson to demonstrate achievement of the lesson objective? This summative evaluation could include a quiz, the construction of a model, the writing of a coherent paragraph, playing a game, completing a worksheet, or any other activity relevant to demonstrating mastery of the objective.

Though you should have considered what instructional accommodations/modifications were necessary during the lesson by addressing the needs described in the diagnosis of your students, you should revisit this issue when you have completed the evaluation of the lesson. If the objective(s) was (were) not achieved by any student, ask yourself if you provided appropriate content, assessment, learning experiences, and materials for that student. Be sure to also ask the students who did not achieve the objective(s) the same questions.

Did you change (with caution) the objective for a student who was *significantly* behind in entry skills for the lesson or offer a series of basic preparatory skills as a foundation for students who did not have the entry skills for the lesson? On the basis of the evaluation, what should you do *now* to ensure the success of any student who did not achieve the lesson objective? And keeping in mind the student's responsibility for his/her own learning, what should that student do now to adjust his/her learning tactic(s) (Popham, 2008)?

14. Follow-up lesson. Once the students have mastered the lesson objective, what will be the next objective they should learn? Communicating this information in advance gives students a sense of purpose and anticipation and could serve as part of the anticipatory set for the subsequent lesson.

15. Other way(s) to teach the lesson. Teachers must be flexible to switch gears, when necessary, as a result of constantly assessing learning during the lesson. In addition, teachers should make it a *regular procedure* to consider different ways to present the same content. Table 5.2 presents the BPOI for lesson planning.

References

Armstrong, T. (2016). *The power of the adolescent brain: Strategies for teaching middle and high school students.* Alexandria, VA: Association for Supervision and Curriculum Development.

Ausubel, D. (1963). *The psychology of meaningful verbal learning.* New York: Grune & Stratton.

Bangert-Drowns, R., Kulik, J., & Kulik, C. (1991). Effects of frequent classroom testing. *Journal of Educational Research, 85,* 88–99.

Beech, M., & Barnitt, V. (2001). *Dealing with differences: Strategies that work.* Audiotape #201174. Alexandria, VA: Association for Supervision and Curriculum Development.

Biggs, J. & Collis, K. (1982). *Evaluating the quality of learning: The SOLO taxonomy.* New York: Academic Press.

Breaden, M. (2008, January 30). Researchers examine importance of learning from "explaining." *Education Week, 27*(21), 5.

Brooks, J., & Brooks, M. (1999). *In search of understanding: The case for constructivist classrooms.* Alexandria, VA: Association for Supervision and Curriculum Development.

Brophy, J. (1988). On motivating students. In D. Berliner & B. Rosenshine (Eds.), *Talks to teachers* (pp. 201–45). New York: Random House.

Bruner, J. (1966). *Toward a theory of instruction.* New York: Norton.

Caine, R. N., & Caine, G. (1994). *Making connections: Teaching and the human brain.* Menlo Park, CA: Addison Wesley.

Castagnera, E., Fisher, D., Rodifer, K., & Sax, C. (1998). *Tools for tailoring individual supports.* In Author, *Deciding what to teach and how to teach it: Connecting students through curriculum and instruction* (pp. 15–18). Colorado Springs, CO: PEAK Parent Center, Inc.

Cavanagh, S. (2008, April 29). Playing games in classroom helping pupils grasp math. *Education Week.* http://www.edweek.org/ew/articles/2008/04/30/35games

Chetty, R., Friedman, J., & Rockoff, J. (2012, January). *The long-term impacts of teachers: Teacher value-added and student outcomes in adulthood* (NBER Working Paper No. 17699, JEL No. I2, J24).

Cotton, K. (2000). *The schooling practices that matter most.* Alexandria, VA: Association for Supervision and Curriculum Development.

Covey, S. (2004). *The 8th habit: From effectiveness to greatness.* New York: Free Press.

Covington, M. (1992). *Making the grade: A self-worth perspective on motivation and school reform.* New York: Cambridge University Press.

Covington, M., & Omelich, C. (1987). "I knew it cold before the exam": A test of the anxiety-blockage hypothesis. *Journal of Educational Psychology, 79,* 393–400.

Csikszentmihalyi, M. (1990). *Flow: The psychology of optimal experience.* New York: Harper & Row.

Danielson, C. (2007). *Enhancing professional practice: A framework for teaching* (2nd ed.). Alexandria, VA: Association for Supervision and Curriculum Development.

Danielson, C. (2016, April 20). Rethinking teacher evaluation. *Education Week, 35*(28), 20, 24.

Danielson, C., & Abrutyn, L. (1997). *An introduction to using portfolios in the classroom.* Alexandria, VA: Association for Supervision and Curriculum Development.

Danielson, C., & McGreal, T. (2000). *Teacher evaluation to enhance professional practice.* Alexandria, VA: Association for Supervision and Curriculum Development.

Deans for Impact (2015). https://deansforimpact.org/resources/the-science-of-learning/

Deci, E., & Ryan, R. (1985). *Intrinsic motivation and self-determination in human behavior.* New York: Plenum.

Delpit, L. (1995). *Other people's children: Cultural conflict in the classroom.* New York: The New Press.

Diamond, M. (1997). *The brain, the mind, and the classroom.* Audiotape #296282. Alexandria, VA: Association for Supervision and Curriculum Development.

Diamond, M., & Hopson, J. (1998). *Magic trees of the mind: How to nurture your child's intelligence, creativity, and healthy emotions from birth through adolescence.* New York: Dutton.

Dweck, C. (2010, January). Mind-sets and equitable education. *Principal Leadership 10*(5), 26–29.

Eisner, E. (1998). *The kinds of schools we need: Personal essays.* Portsmouth, NH: Heinemann.

Elawar, M. C., & Corno, L. (1985). A factorial experiment in teachers' written feedback on student homework: Changing teacher behavior a little rather than a lot. *Journal of Educational Psychology, 77,* 162–173.

Ellis, A. (2001). *Research on educational innovations* (3rd ed.). Larchmont, NY: Eye on Education.

Erwin, J. (2004). *The classroom of choice: Giving students what they need and getting what you want.* Alexandria, VA: Association for Supervision and Curriculum Development.

Ewy, C. (2003). *Teaching with visual frameworks*. Thousand Oaks, CA: Corwin Press.

Felch, J., Song, J., & Poindexter, S. (2010, December 22). In reforming schools, quality of teaching often overlooked. *Los Angeles Times*, p. 4.

Felton, E. (2016, May 12). Are teachers being taught bad science [Web log post]? *Education Week*'s blog. http://blogs.edweek.org/edweek/teacherbeat/2016/05/teachers_are_taught_bad_science.html

Franklin, J. (2005, June). Mental mileage: How teachers are putting brain research to use. *Education Update*, *47*(6). Association for Supervision and Curriculum Development.

Fryshman, B. (2014, August 11). Let's be honest: We don't know how to make great teachers. *Education Week* Online. http://www.edweek.org/tm/articles/2014/08/11/fp_fryshman_teacher_quality.html

Gagne, R. (1977). *The conditions of learning* (3rd ed.). New York: Holt, Rinehart, & Winston.

Gallagher, K. (2010, November 17). Why I will not teach to the test. *Education Week*, *30*(12) 29, 36.

Good, T., & Brophy, J. (1974). Changing teacher and student behavior: An empirical investigation. *Journal of Educational Psychology*, *66*, 390–405.

Hanushek, E. (2011, April 6). Recognizing the value of good teachers. *Education Week*, *30*(27), 34–35.

Haycock, K. (1998). Good teaching matters . . . a lot. *Thinking K–16*, *3*(2), 1–14.

Hook, C., & Rosenshine, B. (1979). Accuracy of teacher reports of their classroom behavior. *Review of Educational Research*, *49*, 1–12.

Hunter, M. (1982). *Mastery teaching*. El Segundo, CA: TIP Publications.

Hunter, M. (1984). *Knowing, teaching, and supervising*. In P. Hosford (Ed.), *Using what we know about teaching* (pp. 169–92). Alexandria, VA: Association for Supervision and Curriculum Development.

Hunter, R. (2004). *Madeline Hunter's mastery teaching: Increasing instructional effectiveness in elementary and secondary schools* (Updated ed.). Thousand Oaks, CA: Corwin Press.

Hyerle, D. (1996). *Visual tools for constructing knowledge*. Alexandria, VA: Association for Supervision and Curriculum Development.

Hyerle, D. (2004). *Student successes with thinking maps*. Thousand Oaks, CA: Corwin Press.

Jensen, E. (1998). *Teaching with the brain in mind*. Alexandria, VA: Association for Supervision and Curriculum Development.

Jensen, E. (2005). *Teaching with the brain in mind* (2nd ed.). Alexandria, VA: Association for Supervision and Curriculum Development.

Joyce, B., & Showers, B. (1995). *Student achievement through staff development* (2nd ed.). New York: Longman.

Joyce, B., & Showers, B. (2002). *Student achievement through staff development* (3rd ed.). Alexandria, VA: Association for Supervision and Curriculum Development.

Joyce, B., Weil, M., with Calhoun, E. (2004). *Models of teaching* (7th ed.). Boston, MA: Pearson.

Kika, F., McLaughlin, T., & Dixon, J. (1992). Effects of frequent testing of secondary algebra students. *Journal of Educational Research*, *85*, 159–62.

Labaree, D. (2008). An uneasy relationship: A history of teacher education in the university. In M. Cochran-Smith, S. Feiman-Nemser, & J. McIntyre (Eds.), *Handbook of research on teacher education: Enduring issues in education* (pp. 290–306).

Lalor, A. (2016). *Ensuring high-quality curriculum: How to design revise or adopt curriculum aligned to student success.* Alexandria, VA: Association for Supervision and Curriculum Development.

Lazear, D. (1998). *The rubrics way: Using MI to assess understanding.* Tucson, AZ: Zephyr Press.

LeDoux, J. (1996). *The emotional brain: The mysterious underpinnings of emotional life.* New York: Simon & Schuster.

Lonsdorf, K. (2017, March 29). A new kind of March madness hits schools. *nprEd, NPR Now Morning Edition.* www.npr.org/sections/ed/2017/03/29/.../a-new-kind-of-march-madness-hits-schools

Marks, M. (2000, January 9). Education Life. *The New York Times*, pp. 16–17.

Marzano, R. J. (2002). *Research-based strategies for increasing student achievement.* Audiotape #203062. Alexandria: VA: Association for Supervision and Curriculum Development.

Marzano, R. J. (2003). *What works in schools?* Alexandria, VA: Association for Supervision and Curriculum Development.

Marzano, R. J. (2007). *The art and science of teaching: A comprehensive framework for effective instruction.* Alexandria, VA: Association for Supervision and Curriculum Development.

Marzano, R. J. (2011, September). Art & science of teaching: The perils and promises of discovery learning. *Educational Leadership, 69*(1), 86–87.

Marzano, R. J. (2017). *The new art and science of teaching.* Bloomington, IN: Solution Tree Press.

Marzano, R. J., & Pickering, D. (2011). *The highly engaged classroom.* Bloomington, IN: Marzano Research Laboratory.

Marzano, R. J., Pickering, D., & Pollock, J. (2001). *Classroom instruction that works: Research-based strategies for increasing student achievement.* Alexandria, VA: Association for Supervision and Curriculum Development.

Mbadu, D. (2008, March 26). The power of parent-teacher relationships. *Teacher Magazine.* http://www.edweek.org/tm/articles/2008/03/26/mbadu_first_web.h19.html?qs=mbadu

McTighe, J., & Wiggins, G. (2004). *Understanding by design: Professional development workbook.* Alexandria, VA: Association for Supervision and Curriculum Development.

Meyer, C. (1992, May). What's the difference between authentic and performance assessment? *Educational Leadership, 49,* 39–40.

Mitchell, R. (1992). *Testing for learning: How new approaches to evaluation can improve American schools.* New York: The Free Press.

Mumford, M., Costanza, D., Baughman, W., Threlfall, V., & Fleishman, E. (1994). Influence of abilities on performance during practice: Effects of massed and distributed practice. *Journal of Educational Psychology, 86,* 134–44.

National Commission on Teaching and America's Future. (1996). *What matters most: Teaching for America's future.* New York: Carnegie Foundation, Author.

Nuthall, G. (1999). The way students learn: Acquiring knowledge from an integrated science and social studies unit. *Elementary School Journal, 99*(4), 303–41.

Nuthall, G., & Alton-Lee, A. (1993). Predicting learning from student experience of teaching: A theory of student knowledge construction in classrooms. *American Educational Research Journal, 30*(4), 799–840.

Nye, B., Konstantopoulos, S., & Hedges, L. (2004, Fall). How large are teacher effects? *Educational Evaluation and Policy Analysis, 26*(3), 237–57.

Oakes, J., & Lipton, M. (2003). *Teaching to change the world* (2nd ed.). New York: McGraw-Hill.

Pagliaro, M. (2012). *Research-based unit and lesson planning: Maximizing student achievement.* Lanham, MD: Rowman & Littlefield.

Pianta, R. (2007, November 6). Measure actual classroom teaching. *Education Week.* www.edweek.org/ew/articles/2007/11/07/11pianta.h27.html

Pipho, C. (1998, January). The value-added side of standards. *Phi Delta Kappan, 79*(5), 341–42.

Popham, W. J. (2008). *Transformative assessment.* Alexandria, VA: Association for Supervision and Curriculum Development.

Popham, W. J. (2011). *Transformative assessment in action: An inside look at applying the process.* Alexandria, VA: Association for Supervision and Curriculum Development.

Ravitch, D. (2003, August 23). A brief history of teacher professionalism. White House Conference on Preparing Tomorrow's Teachers.

Reiman, A., & Thies-Sprinthall, L. (1998). *Mentoring and supervision for teacher development.* New York: Longman.

Rosenthal, R., & Jacobson, L. (1968). *Pygmalion in the classroom.* New York: Holt, Rinehart, & Winston.

Ryan, K., Cooper, J., & Tauer, S. (2008). *Teaching for student learning: Becoming a master teacher.* Boston, MA: Houghton Mifflin.

Sackstein, S. (2016a). Teachers vs educators: Which are you?—Work in progress. http://blogs.edweek.org/teachers/work_in_progress/2016/05/teachers_vs_educators_which_ar.html?intc=main-mpsmcs

Sackstein, S. (2016b, May 26). Student self-assessment practices that work—Work in progress. http://blogs.edweek.org/teachers/work_in_progress/2016/05/student_self-assessment_practi.html

Sadker, M., & Sadker, D. (1994). *Failing at fairness: How America's schools cheat girls.* New York: Scribner.

Salomon, G., & Perkins, D. (1989). Rocky roads to transfer: Rethinking mechanisms of a neglected phenomenon. *Educational Psychologist, 24,* 113–42.

Sanders, W., & Rivers, J. (1996). *Cumulative and residual effects of teachers on future student academic achievement.* Research progress report. Knoxville, TN: University of Tennessee Value-Added Research and Assessment Center.

Scherer, M. (2016, October). Turning lesson plans into learning plans. *Educational Leadership, 74*(2), 7.

Schmoker, M. (2011). *Focus: Elevating the essentials to radically improve student learning.* Alexandria, VA: Association for Supervision and Curriculum Development.

Schneider, J. (2015, April 15). A national strategy to improve the teaching profession. *Education Week,* http://www.edweek.org/ew/articles/2015/04/15/a-national-strategy-to-improve-the-teaching.html

Sousa, D. (2001). *How the brain learns* (2nd ed.). Thousand Oaks, CA: Corwin Press.

Sousa, D. (2006). *How the brain learns* (3rd ed.). Thousand Oaks, CA: Corwin Press.

Stiggins, R. (2002). Assessment crisis: The absence of assessment FOR learning. *Phi Delta Kappan, 83*(10), 758–65.

Stiggins, R. (2005). *Student-involved assessment FOR learning* (4th ed.). Upper Saddle River, NJ: Pearson/Merrill Prentice Hall.

Stiggins, R. (2007, May). Assessment through the student's eyes. *Educational Leadership, 64*(8), 22–26.

Stiggins, R. (2017a). *The perfect assessment system.* Alexandria, VA: Association for Supervision and Curriculum Development.

Stiggins, R. (2017b). *Classroom assessment for student learning: Doing it right-using it well.* Princeton, NJ: Educational Testing Service.

Sylwester, R. (2000). *A biological brain in a cultural classroom: Applying biological research to classroom management.* Thousand Oaks, CA: Corwin Press.

Taggert, G., Phifer, S., Nixon, J., & Wood, M. (1998). *Rubrics: A handbook for construction and use.* Lancaster, PA: Technomic.

Tate, M. (2003). *Worksheets don't grow dendrites: Instructional strategies that engage the brain.* Thousand Oaks, CA: Corwin Press.

Tomlinson, C., & Eidson, C. (2003). *Differentiating in practice: A resource guide for differentiating curriculum, K-5.* Alexandria, VA: Association for Supervision and Curriculum Development.

Tomlinson, C., & McTighe, J. (2006). *Integrating differentiated instruction and understanding by design.* Alexandria, VA: Association for Supervision and Curriculum Development.

Tucker, M. (2016, April 14). How to get a first-rate teacher in front of every student—Top performers. http://blogs.edweek.org/edweek/top_performers/2016/04/how_to_get_a_first-rate_teacher_in_front_of_every_student.html

Webb, N., Alt, M., Ely, R., & Vesperman, B. (2005, July 25). Web alignment tool. Madison, WI: University of Wisconsin, Wisconsin Center of Educational Research.

Weiss, R. (2007, August 6). Gestures convey message: Learning in progress. *The Washington Post,* A06.

Wiener, R. (2016, April 26). Three strategies to improve teacher evaluation. *Education Week, 25*(29), 25, 28.

Wiggins, G. (1996, Spring). Anchoring assessment with exemplars: Why students and teachers need models. *Gifted Child Quarterly, 40*(2), 66–69.

Wiggins, G. (1998). *Educative assessment: Designing assessments to inform and improve student performance.* San Francisco, CA: Jossey-Bass.

Wiggins, G. (2005). *Educative assessment* (2nd ed.). Alexandria, VA: Association for Supervision and Curriculum Development.

Wiggins, G., & McTighe, J. (1998). *Understanding by design.* Alexandria, VA: Association for Supervision and Curriculum Development.

Wiggins, G., & McTighe, J. (2005). *Understanding by design* (2nd ed.). Upper Saddle River, NJ: Prentice Hall.

Wiggins, G., & McTighe, J. (2011). *The understanding by design guide to creating high-quality units.* Alexandria, VA: Association for Supervision and Curriculum Development.

Willingham, D. (2005). Do visual, auditory and kinesthetic learners need visual, auditory, and kinesthetic instruction? Washington, DC: *American Educator, 44*, 31–35.

Willingham, D. (2009). *Why don't students like school?* San Francisco, CA: Jossey-Bass.

Wilcox, J. (2006, February). Less teaching, more assessing. *Education Update, 48*(2), 1–2. Alexandria, VA: Association for Supervision and Curriculum Development.

Wolfe, P. (2001a). *Brain matters: Translating research into classroom practice.* Alexandria, VA: Association for Supervision and Curriculum Development.

Wolfe, P. (2001b). *Brain research: Fad or foundation?* Audiotape #201099. Alexandria, VA: Association for Supervision and Curriculum Development.

Wolfe, P. (2011). Neuroscience reaffirms Madeline Hunter's model. *ASCD Express, 6*(8), 4–5.

Woolfolk, A. (2008). *Educational psychology* (10th ed.). Boston, MA: Pearson.

Wright, S., Horn, S., & Sanders, W. (1997). Teacher and classroom context effects on student achievement: Implications for teacher evaluation. *Journal of Personnel Evaluation in Education, 11*, 57–67.

Young, S. (2014, August). Seven principles of learning better from cognitive science. https://www.scotthyoung.com/blog/2014/08/10/7-principles-learn-better-science/

About the Author

Marie Pagliaro is currently a professional development consultant. She was a full professor and director of the Teacher Education Division at Dominican College, chair of the Education Department at Marymount College, a supervisor of student teachers at Lehman College of the City University of New York, and chair of the Science Department and teacher of chemistry, general science, and mathematics in the Yonkers Public Schools. She received her PhD in curriculum and teaching from Fordham University.

CPSIA information can be obtained
at www.ICGtesting.com
Printed in the USA
BVOW08s0712011117
499221BV00001B/2/P